SNOWBOARDING

SNOWBOARDING

All you need to know about the world's most exhilarating winter sport

JONNO GIBBINS

SMITHMARK

This edition published in 1996 by SMITHMARK Publishers, a division of U.S. Media Holdings, Inc., 16 East 32nd Street, New York, NY 10016.

SMITHMARK books are available for bulk purchase for sales promotion and premium use. For details write or call the manager of special sales, SMITHMARK Publishers, 16 East 32nd Street, New York, NY 10016; (212) 532-6600

First published in Great Britain in 1996 by Parragon Books Limited
Units 13-17
Avonbridge Industrial Estate
Atlantic Road
Avonmouth
Bristol BS11 9QD
United Kingdom

Designed and produced by
Stonecastle Graphics Limited
Old Chapel Studio
Plain Road Marden
Tonbridge, Kent TN12 9LS
United Kingdom

ISBN 0-7651-9699-9

Printed in Italy

Picture credits:

All photos by Jonno Gibbins except for the following: **Burton Snowboards:** 16, 17 (left), 19 (below), 26, 27. **K2 Snowboards:** 17 (top right, below centre & below right), 19 (top), 20, 22, 23, 27 (hats), 29, 77 (left). **Katja Delago:** 11 (top) rider Ring Gerry, 69 (below) rider: Pederzolli Nici. **Amy Truex:** 11 (below). **Touchstone:** 85 (below). Diagram on page 18 by Brian Pearce.

Acknowledgements

I would like to thank the following people for their help while I was putting this book together. Writing a book is not easy and this was my first one, so I couldn't have done it all on my own. So thank you all and I hope that you are around for the next one!
In no particular order:
Amy Truex for her scathing but constructive technical edits, for riding in my instructional sequences and for organizing my photos. Amy is a Certified PSIA Snowboard Instructor, currently working at Donner Ski Ranch, California. ❊ Todd Beane for changing all the English to American and correcting my grammar. ❊ Andre and Margaret Mazur for providing me with a killer house for the winter. ❊ Collier Cooke and Becki Moore at Ski Homewood. ❊ Audi Quattro for powering me through all those snow drifts. ❊ Dana and Chris from Ernesto for supplying clothing. ❊ Nick Perata for his extreme words and riding skills. ❊ Ian Trotter for telling Paul Turner that I might have time to write a book!

Thanks to the following Riders:

Pat Meurier	Amy Truex
Colt Wymore	Cammeron Beck
Tyler Lepore	Wade Wheeler
John Enloe	Matt Enloe
Nate Mohorco	Annie Remmers
Spencer Tamblyn	Steve Sneddon
Kyle Frankland	Dave O'Day
Johan Olaffson	

Also:

Donner Ski Ranch (Don Bostick)
K2 Snowboards (Martin Robinson)
Steamboat Springs, Colorado, USA
Brighton, Utah, USA

11,99

Contents

Introduction by Nick Perata   6

The History of Snowboarding   8

The Conflict Between Snowboarding & Skiing   12

Everybody's Doing It!   14

Equipment Types & Uses   16

Clothing Types & Styles   24

Different Disciplines   30

Techniques – How to . . .   36

The Competition Circuit   74

Buying New & Used Equipment   76

Equipment Care & Servicing   78

Where to Snowboard   82

Fitness   84

Safety & Rules of the Slopes   88

The Future of Snowboarding   90

Glossary   92

Useful Addresses   95

Index   96

Introduction

When I began snowboarding in 1983-4, the boards were fairly primitive – no steel edges, just fins and skegs. Snowboarding didn't even seem like a proper sport then, because only a handful of enthusiasts were involved in it, having made a natural crossover from skateboarding to the snow.

At that time there was a lack of snowboarding equipment and we could only ride the back country, because dedicated skiers and ski resorts didn't want to know about this new sport – they didn't understand it and would not allow it at the resorts.

Snowboarding has changed dramatically since then, particularly in the way that products have developed and evolved and with the use of high-tech materials that enable designers to produce boards that perform with optimum precision.

Product innovation has been chiefly responsible for the evolution of snowboarding, which has allowed riders to raise the level of their individual ability as well as taking the sport to an entirely new level.

Now snowboarding is much easier to learn than it used to be, with the advent of boards, bindings, boots and other equipment all specifically designed for the beginner – which allows you to enjoy the pleasure without the pain! Now it probably takes the beginner a week to reach the same level of competence that it took me a month to achieve in those early days.

In recent years, so many areas of good snow have been made available for snowboarding that accessibility to easy riding terrain is now virtually unlimited.

After all these years I am still involved with snowboarding on an everyday basis – and every day is different! There is an indescribable feeling that you get when you ride your snowboard, when you learn and when you excel. Everybody gets that feeling, whatever level you are at. Then there is the feeling of being in the mountains – every time I strap that board to my feet, the same buzz is there, even after all these years! Also, with the advantage of experience, at this point in my career I know that I am going to be doing sweet lines in deep powder!

Why should anyone take up this sport? It can be an outlet for the stress of modern life; it can give you inner strength and make you feel good about yourself, by doing something that is so easy. The sheer thrill of just moving down a slope is reason enough to go out and do it.

Snowboarding can be effortless and anyone who tries it and gives a little time and patience will be hooked. And everybody can learn to snowboard, at any age – I have seen six year old snowboarders and over 90 year old snowboarders.

The best advice to a beginner is to take a lesson from a qualified instructor, who will show you how to snowboard correctly. Next, ensure that you have the correct equipment – the right size of boots, the right board for your weight and height and the right size of clothes, in fact, everything should fit you perfectly. If you don't use the right gear you will make learning the necessary skills more difficult. Also, reading books and magazines and watching videos about snowboarding will help you to understand the sport more and will give you the edge to succeed.

I suggest that if you are new to snowboarding, buy a used board of the correct size to bang around and become good on. Once you are competent, go ahead and buy a new board, then with the best equipment you can afford you will progress quickly.

What about the future? There are no limits to snowboarding as far as tricks are concerned, but I think the number of products and manufacturers caught up in the current over exposure of the sport will diminish over the next few years, leaving just a few large, well organized companies, similar to the situation with skiing.

The popularity of snowboarding will continue to increase, with more people taking up the sport as they appreciate the ease of getting started and the fun to be had for all ages. As equipment develops and improves, so will riders' abilities.

In general people are going to be both skiing and snowboarding more, and the beauty of snowboarding is that it allows riders to enjoy their sport in all conditions, from ice to powder, slush and bumps.

The baggy clothes and 'grunge' appearance that have become an image statement for snowboarding will fade away as the sport matures, and the conflicts with skiing, which are already diminishing, will disappear as it gains respect.

A generation of the sport has grown up already and now the next generation of young riders are active. Freeriding, hiking and back country offers a new challenge to experienced snowboarders, allowing them the freedom of terrain that is so different to designated ski areas.

Finally we are to be involved in the Olympics. Snowboarding is a legitimate alpine event with GS, Slalom and half pipe, but it needs the involvement of active snowboarders, rather than just the product manufacturers, at the very highest levels to ensure that it continues to be a worthy Olympic sport.

With top riders at the forefront of organization and control, snowboarding will make a spectacular Olympic event – I only wish that this had happened years ago, so that I could have had the opportunity to be involved!

There are still some ski areas that only allow snowboarding during official competitions and not at other times. This discrimination against the sport segregates skiers and snowboarders and does both a disservice. Only by working together, will both of these exciting winter sports continue to flourish. Each needs the other and there should be a cross over of information, techniques and fun.

Like other sports, snowboarding will give you a feeling of achievement as you gain confidence, test your ability and learn – not only about technique but also about yourself. In this fast changing winter sport you never stop learning – I am still learning, and as I observe what kids are inventing and creating in snowboarding, I am keen to do the same. Take your time to learn and take your bruises!

Use snowboarding as an opportunity – an opportunity to travel, to escape the pressures at home, school or work. Snowboarding can make you feel more 'laid back' and relaxed than traditional skiing, and as can be seen by the increasing numbers of riders, it is easy to learn.

Be patient – nobody ever learned to snowboard overnight. Don't give up if success does not happen immediately; take that first lesson, learn how to fall as well as learning how to ride, and you are less likely to hurt yourself. Only quit having lessons when you feel comfortable getting off the lifts, making heel and toe edge turns, stopping and you are totally in control of your board.

Nick Perata

Nick Perata is one of the World's most accomplished snowboarders to have emerged from the early eighties. He is a top rider and instructor and has starred in numerous snowboarding movies and magazines. He has appeared as the featured rider in a Lucozade commercial and has undertaken many complex and technically demanding rides, including being the first snowboarder to ride the Great North Chute, a 1500ft, 50 degree vertical chute in the Bridger Mountain Range, southern Montana.

Nick has successfully ridden off both the 1200ft summit of the Mooses Tooth and the 1100ft peak of Mount Spur in Alaska.

He is a snowboarding consultant and event organizer, as well as being vice president and founder of Alaska Heliboard Adventures.

The History of Snowboarding

Snowboarding is the World's fastest growing winter sport and with participation increasing by 50% in 1994, projected figures suggest that by the year 2000, there will be as many snowboarders as skiers on our mountains.

So where did they all come from?

Well, contrary to popular belief, snowboarding is not an off-shoot of skiing, but was developed independently and many years ago.

From drawings and texts found in Scandinavia, Siberia and Central Asia, scientists can tell us that skis have been used for thousands of years for transportation, hunting and fighting. In a Swedish peat bog, archaeologists discovered a short, wide ski which was estimated to be about 4,500 years old.

Perhaps this was the very first snowboard, who knows! If so, this early prototype was kept under wraps for a few more years – early pioneers probably decided to wait until ski resorts would allow them on their lifts!

Regardless of early man's efforts, snowboarding is hardly 'new'. Conceived in the '60s and '70s, snowboarding grew up in the '80s and is commonplace at most ski areas in the '90s. There was no sudden 'jump' in popularity, but rather a long, deliberate growth, nurtured by a few pioneering companies and now exploited by many.

It all started in 1963 when a certain Tom Sims designed the 'ski board' as part of an eighth grade woodshop Christmas project in New Jersey, USA. Three years after Sims had designed the snowboard, Sherman Poppen came out with the 'Snurfer', which he initially invented for his kids by bolting two skis together. The snurfer was patented by Poppen and sold like hot cakes as snow-surfing took off across the USA. On February 18th, 1968, the World's first Snurfer competition was held, at Blackhouse Hill in Muskegon, Michigan. The race was straight downhill and the winner was the fastest over the finish line in one piece!

In 1969, a young Jake Burton Carpenter received a Snurfer as a Christmas gift – his snowboarding passion was born as were the two most famous names-to-be in the sport. Sims and Burton.

Snowboarding now includes many disciplines.

In 1970, East coast surfer, Dimitrije Milovich, had the idea of making snowboards after sliding around on cafeteria trays in upstate New York. Dimitrije designed and tested boards in the Utah backcountry producing swallowtail fish shapes that would later become the 'Winterstick'. In 1971 he patented his idea but declined to enforce his patent with other companies even though it didn't expire until 1988.

Also attempting to patent this new innovation at this time was Bob Weber. Weber designed a 'Skiboard' along with bindings and was granted a patent in 1972.

Using design techniques developed for skateboards, surfboards and, more importantly, skis, these early snowboards have evolved into the highly technical equipment that we know today.

However, it was never as simple as all that. Newcomers to the sport today are unaware of the struggle that snowboarders went through to have their passion recognised as a sport and not simply a menace to society. In the early days of the 1980s, none of the ski resorts would allow 'snowskis' on their hill, so 'boarders would have to hike into the backcountry to ride and to research and develop their new designs. Thus most of the riding was done in powder and soft snow – one early misconception with the general public was that snowboards were only good in powder.

By the mid-eighties, snowboarding was beginning to lose some of its fad image and was depicted less as an 'underground' activity and more of a mainstream sport, popular with more than just a few backcountry surfers. Thus began the fight to be recognised as a sport and to be accepted at every ski area.

As the ski areas opened up, so the contests could begin. In 1987 the first World Championships took place in Livigno, Italy and at Breckenridge in the US. Around this time, snowboarding began a surge of popularity in Europe, on the back of a declining skateboard industry. Jose Fernandes was Europe's first pioneer, winning many races all over the world and developing the plate binding, specific to snowboard racing.

A certain attitude began to surface on either side of the pond. In America, as their background was in surfing and skating, so snowboarders developed the freestyle side of the sport, using flexible bindings and soft boots for the necessary freedom. Conversely, European snowboarders came from the sport of skiing and brought with them ski boots, stiff race boards and the need for speed. As a result, early International competitions resulted in Euro's winning all the races and the Yanks winning the freestyle events.

With its roots in surfing and skateboarding, snowboarding has until recently attracted groups of youngsters who would not normally have been interested in winter snow sports.

They brought with them their own fashion, culture and attitude, which unfortunately projected a young and rebellious image.

As most resorts now allow snowboarding, it has developed a high profile with skiers and the media and has seen much bad publicity as the more traditional members of the ski industry tried to halt its rapid growth. However, as more and more skiers cross over to snowboarding and enjoy its faster learning curve and its limitless possibilities for enjoyment, snowboarding is losing its rebellious image and is forming a more solid infrastructure on which to grow into a major sport recognised in every household worldwide.

Its versatility is a major attraction. There are different sports and disciplines within snowboarding itself, which will be covered in detail later in this book.

Left: Most early snowboarding was done in powder and soft snow, in the backcountry.
Above: International competitions are now very popular, and professional, events.
Below: The author, Jonno Gibbins, was one of the infamous 'Euro-carvers' and became British Slalom Champion in 1990.

The Conflict Between Snowboarding & Skiing

Until the mid '80s, snowboarding was basically unheard of at the major ski resorts and therefore not allowed. Because it was an unknown entity, there was much fear and concern on the part of the authorities and traditional skiers, resulting in an alarming conflict between all snow users. As many pioneering snowboarders will recall, even the sports name was often changed to become; skiboarding, tobogganing, mono-boarding, board-skiing, snow-surfing, snurfing, snowballing . . . and no doubt there have been others!

One of the reasons that snowboarding was not accepted for many years as a sport in itself and as a respectable pastime, was that it was considered a 'Fad', similar to skateboarding in that it would not last as a sport popular with the masses. When something 'different' comes along and challenges the existence of a major sport such as skiing, there is bound to be a conflict. So what makes snowboarding so different?

As the sport was created, not as a mode of transport, but as an art form, it has evolved as an expression of personality, freedom, grace and fun. It is something very different from the normality of skiing and has added excitement and endless possibilities.

Therefore, depending on whether alpine or freestyle oriented, snowboarders will use the available terrain to its limits. The groomed slopes are not simply a 'road' for reaching the bottom of the mountain, they are a canvas on which to create expressions of movement and fluidity. Freestylers will use all the available banks and jumps on the slopes as well as the powder and other 'off-piste' possibilities, and the alpine 'boarders will use the groomed slopes for carving graceful turns at speed. Snowboarders do have a problem with flatter sections of the slope as they are not equipped with poles with which to push themselves along. They therefore stay away from these areas whenever possible. Long, flat traverses are also not easy for the fledgling snowboarder, neither are large mogul fields. Compared to skiing though, powder can be handled after only a few days of snowboarding, which opens up the whole mountain to the snowboarder and provides an experience of indescribable proportions. As a snowboard is much wider than two skis, it affords much more floatation in deep snow and thus more speed, control and manoeuvrability than skis. Being able to experience the adrenaline rush of snowboarding in powder is one of its major attractions.

Snowboarders will use the available terrain to its limits and freestylers will use any banks and jumps on the slopes as well as on the powder and other 'off-piste' areas. This sometimes creates conflicts with more traditional skiers.

The difference in the two sports' mentality is also very clear. Skiing was traditionally a 'gentleman's' sport for the rich upper classes. Although this has changed dramatically in recent years as holiday companies and ski areas have made skiing accessible to all classes and pockets, the underlying attitudes remain stagnant and demure. This mentality is very apparent with the controllers and authorities concerned with the sport of skiing, who have grown up with their sport from its traditional beginning as a military and aristocratic past-time.

Snowboarding, probably due to its surfing and skateboarding roots, is a very free and relaxed sport. Thus it encourages people with a surf type attitude (laid back and casual) to enjoy the sport for its fun content, not because it provides a status symbol. The sport is new, creative and exciting and attracts people with the enthusiasm and ability to cope with such an experience. Many people beginning snowboarding do so because they are searching for new limits and horizons and are bored with their skiing progress which has reached a plateau.

As snowboarding continues to grow at an amazing rate, so those ski areas that originally declined to allow the sport, now actively promote snowboarding and provide the necessary specialist facilities such as parks and half pipes. Ski areas, ski manufacturers and all others involved with the ski industry can no longer ignore the presence of snowboarding – figures categorically show that the number of snowboarders on the ski slopes is fast catching the number of skiers. And it's not just new snowboarders – many skiers are crossing over.

Powder can be handled after only a relatively few days of snowboarding practice.

It would seem that the most outspoken anti-snowboarders have either never tried the sport or have simply had a bad experience concerning snowboarding. It is a fact that many skiers who try snowboarding are so hooked that they never return to skiing. It may be true that they would never have become expert skiers, perhaps due to the lack of time or ability, but can become proficient snowboarders due to its fast learning curve.

Snowboards are not toys. They are highly technical winter sports equipment, and should be treated accordingly. All beginners should take lessons in snowboarding and in slope etiquette.

Snowboarding is not a fad – it is here to stay.

Everybody's Doing It!

So, what exactly is a snowboarder, what do they look like, how does one become a snowboarder – what are the necessary credentials?

In general, snowboarders are thought of as baggy pant wearing, bright haired, body pierced punk type guys with nothing better to do than terrorize the ski slopes scaring skiers half to death.

Is this true? Of course not. Snowboarding has become a sport that is popular across a wide cross-section of the population and there is no prerequisite for age, occupation or gender.

Skiing is no longer attracting the younger generation as it used to as it is now seen as the less exciting of the two main snow sports. The majority of skiers are now in the 28+ age range (American Sports Data Demographics – ASDD) while the younger age group are

crossing over to snowboarding. The majority of youngsters now beginning snow sports take up snowboarding – it is seen as *the* sport to be doing, is more exciting and quicker to learn with more opportunities to achieve a high proficiency level.

What about the rest of us? Well, snowboarding has an extremely steep learning curve. In English, that means that within a few days, a novice snowboarder can progress as far, if not further, than a learner skier would in a number of weeks. In fact, most beginner students advance to an intermediate level after their first lesson – about one and a half hours! How long does it take the average skier to learn how to ski powder? Years. But, on a snowboard, the average snowboarder can be producing exhilarating, arcing powder turns after a matter of days. Being able to feel that you are progressing quickly at a sport is the key to staying interested and motivated to learn. Many skiers only go to the mountains a few times a season and never really progress – they actually regress during the off period and then spend their vacation week re-learning, to reach their previous level.

Snowboarders also regress during the down time but re-learning is rather more rapid than skiing.

Originally, snowboarding was a totally male oriented sport, not appealing to females at all. Now, girls that do try snowboarding are invariably surprised at its ease and that it doesn't take excessive muscle and brawn to become proficient. In the late '80s it was rare to see any girls snowboarding. Last season saw the emergence of signature boards built specifically for girls and clothing designed to fit the female body, making the sport so much

easier and more welcoming for the fairer sex. Now, the 1995/96 season brings us ski slopes with almost as many female as males – and that can't be a bad thing! In fact, having more women involved in the sport will help to further release it from the stranglehold of its 'bad-boy' image.

In any given ski area this season, there will be an impressive cross-section of generations tearing up the slopes on snowboards, from 4 year olds riding purpose built 1 metre boards to their parents and even grandparents enjoying carving on all-terrain snowboards.

Equipment Types & Uses

Ski equipment has been in the design process for many years and is now being made at a highly precise level with advanced materials and technology. Snowboard designers have been able to borrow a lot of design ideas from these ski companies and have now pushed design techniques even further so that snowboards are now built to an even higher degree of technicality than skis. These rapid advances are also partly due to the help of Computer Aided Design (CAD) and the use of dedicated and professional Research and Development (R & D) teams.

BOARDS

Snowboards have a similar construction to that of skis, with wood or foam cores, vertical or horizontal lamination, carbon & kevlar reinforcement, varied flex patterns, steel wrap around edges, P-Tex bases, protected tips and tails and now also some mono-block construction (one piece wrap-over top sheet incorporating the side wall thus giving added strength).

Snowboards are now designed for every possible type of riding and every type of rider. The beginner snowboarder will feel quite daunted when realising the number of 'boards available and will probably be totally confused as to what they need. Although the vast amount of product in the shops may seem to make decisions harder, it actually makes life super easy and advances individual riding skills extremely rapidly, compared to a few years ago. Why? Well, today, one can find a snowboard specifically designed for ones own weight, height, level of

ability, sex, preferred discipline, price range and colour taste!

There are boards designed for: half pipe, slope style, freeriding, powder, slalom, giant slalom, extreme riding, women and children. There are also many boards designed to cross over a couple of the disciplines therefore

giving greater versatility and providing more value for money to the customer who does not want to restrict themselves to one aspect of the sport but does not want to purchase three boards either.

Snowboards are now available in a bewildering assortment of shapes, sizes, styles and colours. However, you will have no problem getting fitted for your specific requirements at a reputable snowboard store. (Burton Snowboards)

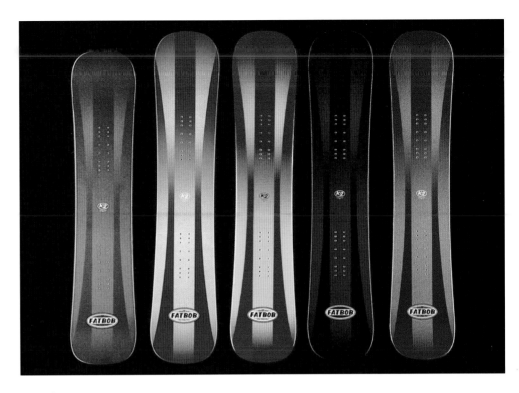

Fatbobs revolutionized the snowboard industry in 1993. (K2 Snowboards)

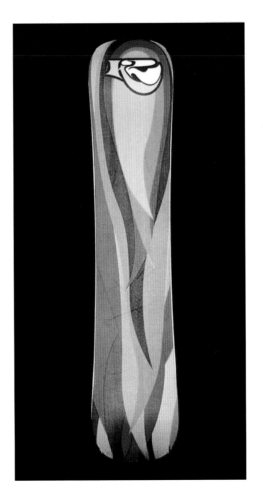

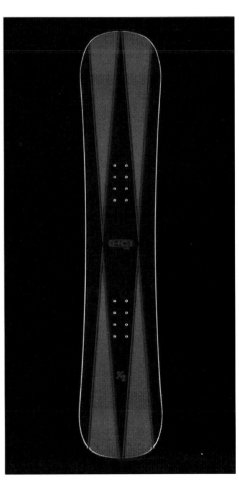

The Zeppelin. (K2 Snowboards)   *The HC. (K2 Snowboards)*

BOARD DESIGN SPECIFICS

Snowboards are designed to perform in various types of snow conditions for many types of people. There are certain characteristics of the board that are altered to create the different boards.

Side Cut

The radius of the side cut helps to determine the turning ability of the board. The larger the radius, the larger the turn, the smaller the radius, the smaller the turn.

Snowboards are designed for specific uses and can be tailored to suit the individual.

Flex

The stiffness of the board is combined with the side cut radius to create the correct turning specifics that allow boards to perform a variety of functions. In general, race and carving boards have a stiffer flex as they are designed for harder snow conditions and need extra grip in icy conditions, and stiffer boards perform better at higher speeds. Freestyle boards require a softer flex to enable the board to ollie, take off and land in complete control. Freestyle boards have large side cut radius' (virtually no side cut) as they are not designed for fast turns – the width enhances the stability of the board for freestyle disciplines.

Camber

Combined with the side cut and the flex, the camber is essential to creating the required ride characteristics. As pressure is applied to the boards edge beneath the feet (where the camber is greatest), the board bends to create an opposite camber thus performing the turn. The radius of the sidecut will then determine the radius of the carved turn. More camber along with a stiffer flex will create a board with a dynamic turning ability which will, however, need to be ridden with extra power and aggression – such boards are found in the alpine racing arena. Most boards are made with a little less camber and a softer flex to create a more forgiving ride.

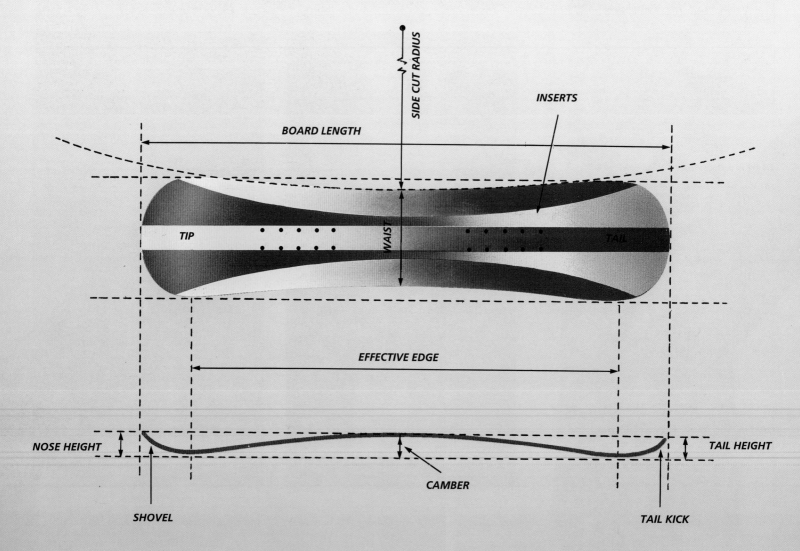

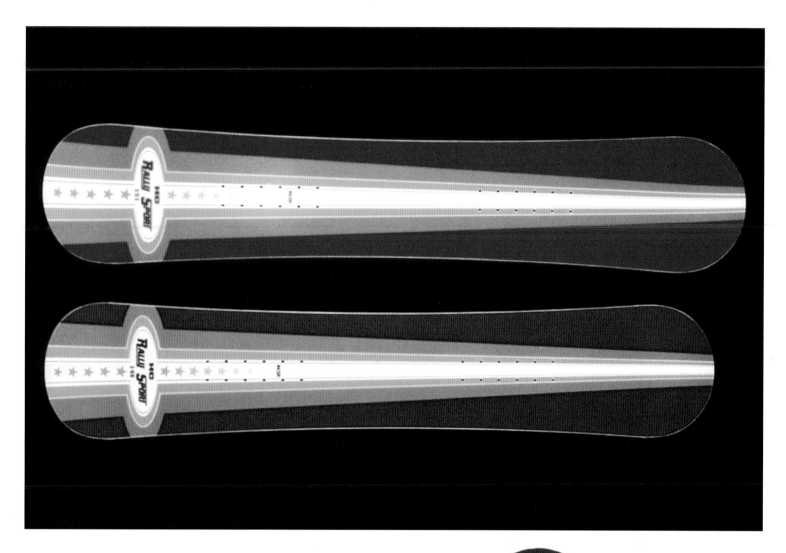

Above: Introduced in 1996, the HC Ralley Sport is a snowboard designed specifically for the price-conscious freestyler. (K2 Snowboards)

Nose Shovel and Tail Kick

Race and alpine boards have a small shovel and little or no tail kick as they are designed for hard snow and require as much board as possible in contact with the ground to achieve maximum control. Freestyle boards have much more shovel and tail kick, depending on the specific design. Freeriding boards have a longer more drawn out shovel and a smaller tail kick, while half pipe boards are generally twin tipped, meaning that each end of the board is shaped the same way.

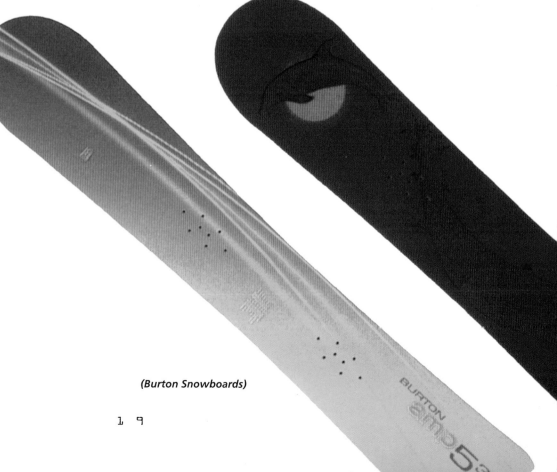

(Burton Snowboards)

Effective Edge

This is the section of the edge that is in contact with the snow, the part of the edge that works to control the board. The more edge that is in contact with the snow, the more control the rider has over the board. Older boards were designed with large nose and tail up-turn and thus little effective edge, making them long and clumsy. With less nose and tail up-turn, shorter boards can be made to perform better than older, longer boards with the same effective edge.

Base and Edges

All boards are produced with a 'P-Tex' base also found on skis. This plastic is made in varying grades of density with lower density being the most common. (1000 & 2000). In general, high tech race boards are made with a higher grade to produce higher speeds. P-Tex bases dry out very easily and should be waxed in order to prolong a boards life to maintain its gliding ability on the snow – a poorly maintained base will 'stick' on wet snow and be very difficult to ride as well as unpleasant. All boards are also produced with steel edges similar to skis. These edges are essential for controlling the board in hard snow and icy conditions and should be regularly sharpened.

The Waist

This is the measurement taken at the narrowest point across the board between the side cut of the two edges. A narrower waist is common on race boards – these boards being altogether narrower are able to be turned from edge to edge more rapidly than freestyle boards which are wider throughout.

The Tail

Tail shape differs again depending on the boards use. Alpine boards have a square shape to maintain maximum edge contact, freestyle boards are rounded for riding transitions and performing ground based tricks. Pure powder boards have a V shaped swallow-tail which is designed to sink in powder therefore bringing the nose out of the deep snow in order to enhance its floating capabilities, and also to create a softer flexing tail that can be used also on the hard packed groomed slopes.

Right: Whatever your snowboarding passion, you will be able to find a board that is designed to get the best out of the terrain and help to improve your performance. It is essential that your board is well maintained if you expect to achieve optimum results.

Below left: The Dart Swinger is a popular snowboard for smaller riders and kids and is designed specifically for the lighter weight, smaller footed riders. The Eldorado, below, is recommended for big mountains and deep powder. (K2 Snowboards)

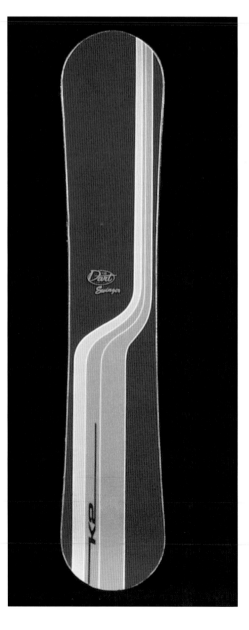

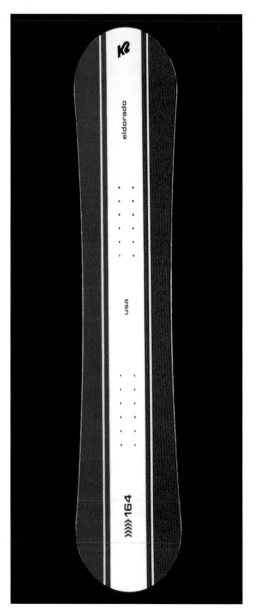

BOOTS

Skiers obviously use hard shell boots which are very necessary to give precise control over the skis. Many recreational skiers, who perhaps only ski for one or two weeks during the season, do not own their own boots and therefore have to rent once in the resort. There are always complaints and problems associated with poorly fitting and painful ski boots — one of the attractions of snowboarding is that the boots used are necessarily much softer and more flexible than ski boots and consequently more comfortable. In snowboarding there are two distinct types of boot, commonly referred to as 'hard' and 'soft'. The soft boots are used for freestyle and freeriding and were originally adapted for use from Canadian type snow boots (although they are technically rather more advanced these days!), offering a great deal of comfort and maximum flexibility for freestyle tricks. Hard boots (much more flexible than ski boots with added forward, lateral and medial flex) are used for alpine freeriding and racing, where a greater degree of control and response is necessary.

Freestyle binding.

Freeride binding.

Rugged all-mountain boot.

Super lightweight freestyle boot.

Semi-stiff, fully supportive boot.

(All pictures: K2 Snowboards)

All-mountain boot.

BINDINGS

The main difference between snowboard and ski bindings, and the one that gives skiers most cause for concern, is that ski bindings release when the skier takes a heavy fall, but snowboard bindings do not. As skiers have a ski on each foot, when they fall, it is possible to receive injuries from twisting knees and ankles as the two skis rotate independently. Therefore ski bindings need to release to prevent nasty injuries. However, as a snowboarder has both feet fixed to one board, the legs cannot twist as easily and knee and ankle twisting injuries are therefore not as common. In order to use releasable bindings on a snowboard, it would be necessary to ensure that they both release together and also that there is a satisfactory braking system to stop the board running away after releasing.

Most boards are manufactured with metal inserts in which to locate the chosen bindings. These inserts are rock solid and can be used in any manner such that the rider is positioned in their optimum snowboarding position. A few boards are still made with an aluminium top sheet which is drilled into and self tapping screws are then used to attach the bindings. The drawback with this situation is that the bindings cannot then be easily moved, as the rider, the riders ability or the riding conditions change.

There are three types of snowboard bindings.

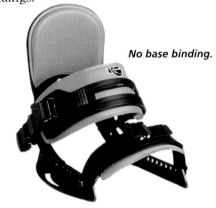

No base binding.

Freestyle

Also called 'soft'. These bindings are constructed with a high back and with two or three straps over the foot and ankle. There are different types of soft binding, including two strap for freestyle, three strap for freeriding, and baseless for extra board 'feel' in freestyle.

Alpine

Also called 'hard' bindings. These are used with hard boots primarily for racing and free-carving. More rigid for precision control at high speed. Steeper angled stance positions are necessary as hard boots flex less laterally than soft boots and to prevent toe and heel overhang on narrower race boards.

Step-in

New this season in the stores and the latest innovation in snowboard binding design, this system uses the common freestyle binding and boot combination but with the ability to simply step into the binding and release with one touch – no more uncomfortable and awkward straps. Could this be the future of snowboard bindings? The ride produced offers extra precise control on the ground and super tweakability in the air.

   With step-in bindings comes the end of the wet-butt syndrome. No more sitting down to adjust straps, no more foot pain and the ability to click-in on the chair and ride off!

Right and far right: This could be the binding system of the future – a quick, comfortable way to step into a precision made binding. (K2 Snowboards)

All-round 'Clicker' soft boot.

Freestyle step-in boot.

New 'Clicker' binding.

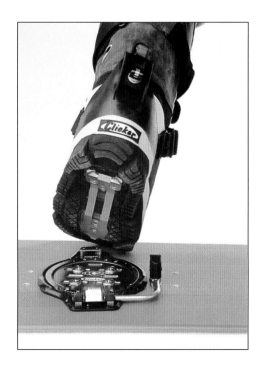

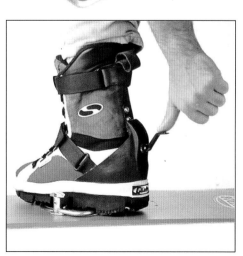

Clothing Types & Styles

Just because some nutty 12 year old jibber decides to snowboard in a snow storm wearing jeans and a T-shirt, it doesn't mean that this is considered optimum snowboard garb for bad weather conditions. How do kids manage to stay warm in T-shirts? It must have something to do with the metabolism at that age . . .

Gone are the days of close fitting, one piece, fluorescent ski suits and in their place are baggy jackets and pants. Popular colours now tend to be more earthy and less bright than the early days when ski clothing was all that was available. There are many embarrassing photos out there, especially in Europe where fluoro was very much 'in' during snowboardings adolescence. There have been all sorts of anti snowboarding quips in the past and clothing has taken much abuse. But there is a functional reason for snowboard specific clothing to be big and baggy. Snowboarders do not move the same way as skiers. Snowboarding requires the rider to make dynamic and aggressive movements that would be restricted by tight clothing. The earthy colours also reflect the snowboarders more laid back and down-to-earth approach to life.

So, what should you look for when buying for your wardrobe? When deciding what to purchase, take into consideration where, when and how much you are going to ride. All ski areas of the world have differing climates and snow conditions.

It's important to remember that weather conditions in the mountains can change in a matter of minutes, from hot and sunny to freezing and windy. So be prepared. Always carry your beanie and neck warmer in a

pocket, just in case. Layering your clothing is also the key, rather than wearing one very warm jacket. It is better to be too hot than too cold. At least if you are hot, you can take off the top layer, or open a couple of vents. If you are too cold, you just have to head back to the lodge as quickly as possible for a hot chocolate, while the well prepared rage in the powder. On a more serious note, cold kills. Be prepared for the worst that mother nature can offer.

Right: Snowboarding clothing should be big and baggy, to allow maximum freedom when manoeuvring. It is also essential to be warm as well as comfortable.

Below: This young snowboarder is keeping warm, and fashionable, while having a good time. There is no point in suffering for your sport – wear plenty of loose layers and don't forget that hat!

A good selection of snowboard clothing (Burton Snowboards) and hats (K2 Snowboards).

Let's start at the beginning.

FIRST LAYER – Otherwise known as thermals. This layer is essential to winter warmth. Some snowboard clothing companies make a first layer, but there really is no such thing as a snowboard specific thermal! Any generic brand will do! Thermal shirts with a roll neck are a good choice – keeping cold air and snow out of your neck area is well advisable.

FLEECE/SWEATER – Fleece is one of the warmest clothing materials that you can buy. Fleece pullovers are highly recommended as the next layer of clothing and are available in different thicknesses and weights. Loose fitting is important. In the spring time, when it's too warm for your jacket, all you need is a fleece. Top of the range fleeces are lined with wind proof material for extra warmth. If not fleece, go for a warm sweater – again lined sweaters are available to combat wind chill. A thick hooded sweatshirt is the next best on the list.

JACKETS – These come in various shapes and sizes, some pullover, some with a full length front zip. That's personal preference. What you do need to look for is a jacket with a long back (tail), preferably made from a more durable material in this area.

Remember that you are going to be sitting in the snow a lot during your snowboarding life, whether beginner or expert. It's a fact of life, we have to rest sometime! Also look for a large fit, underarm vents, a high collar and/or removable hood. Some top of the line jackets come with a removable liner of some kind, often fleece, that helps to keep you warm on those powder days and can be worn without the jacket in the spring time. Lighter weight jackets are a good buy – not as well insulated as the top range versions, but you can wear extra layers underneath and still be as warm. They are also less expensive and more practical in warmer spring conditions.

PANTS – Again, loose fitting is important. Look for bib and braces or a high cut waist for powder conditions. A reinforced butt area is a very good idea, as are strengthened knees. Make sure that the pants are long enough and have a built in gaiter that covers your boot uppers to keep the snow out. Try them on with your boots before you buy. Side vents are a good idea for spring time – full length side zips mean that you can lie out at the mountain top restaurant and work on your tan!!

GLOVES – Your hands come into contact with the snow much more than in skiing, and you are constantly adjusting bindings and carrying around snowboards with sharp edges. So you need a sturdy pair of gloves made from a durable material, that are somewhat waterproof and breathable. Some are made with removable wrist supports that may be a good idea for your beginner stage. A removable liner is a good feature, making drying the gloves easier. Gloves that extend above your wrists and can be tightened with a draw string over your jacket cuffs are ideal – preventing snow from sneaking up your sleeves. If you have poor circulation in your hands, consider using mitts for added warmth. Or try a combination glove/mitt that leaves your thumb and first finger free for those minor adjustments.

HATS/NECK WARMERS – Perhaps the most under-rated piece of clothing is the fleece neck warmer. If you've never worn one, you don't know what you are missing. Perhaps you've seen them in the stores and thought that they were too kookie? Well they keep you ultra warm and fend off that unwanted snow. Don't tell me that you enjoy the sensation of snow trickling down your neck?!

Don't forget your head – most of the body's heat is lost through the head, so wear a beanie of some kind. There are hundreds of choices, from wool to fleece, from plain skull caps to brightly coloured, outrageous jester hats. Don't leave home without one.

ACCESSORIES

Apart from the obvious equipment such as board, bindings, boots and something to wear, is there anything else that you will need for your new life as a snowboarder?

Actually, yes. There is a plethora of bits and pieces out there to satisfy your every need. Some items are very necessary and some are simply gimmicks. Here's a selection of the more indispensable.

SUNGLASSES – A must in any weather. When conditions are sunny, the added glare from the snow can really damage your eyes if they are not protected. Always wear a good pair of sunglasses and make sure that they cut out 100% of the Ultra Violet rays. Even when the skies are overcast, UV rays still penetrate the clouds – on these occasions, use glasses that are less tinted. In bad light, use a yellow or orange lens to help visibility. Glasses also stop your eyes from streaming at high speeds. Do not wear sunglasses with glass lenses – there is a possibility that they could break on impact and damage your eyes. Plastic lenses are safer and lighter. Stay away from metal frames too – again if they snap during a fall, the metal arm can do much facial damage.

SUNGLASS SAVERS – Some sunglasses grip to your head well, some don't. There are many types of Spec Savers available and they all do the same job. Some people love them and some hate them.

GOGGLES – For poor weather conditions goggles are essential. When it is snowing, windy and cold, goggles will give you good visibility and keep your face warm. More expensive goggles have a double lens plus other

Above: Goggles will give you good visibility and keep your face warm, even when the weather conditions are clear, but very cold.

anti-fog features for clear vision at all times. Even when conditions are clear but it is very cold, wearing goggles is recommended to help stay warm. Various removable lenses are available for different conditions. Use yellow or orange for low light and reflective for sunny conditions. Try not to take them on and off all the time while you are riding – they are guaranteed to fog up.

LENS CLOTH – Carry one every time you ride. As you know, you are going to fall and you are going to dump your head, covering your glasses or goggles with snow. There's only one way to clean the lenses efficiently and that's with a lens cloth.

SUN SCREEN – Perhaps obvious, but nevertheless, people forget. At high altitudes the air is thinner and thus the sun can burn quicker. It is very important to use a high factor sun screen, at least SPF 15. Many people use SPF 50 – don't worry, you will still be tanned by the end of the week. Use a sunscreen that is waterproof, sweatproof and rub proof. You don't want it running into your eyes and you don't want to rub it off. Carry a small tube with you at all times – even if you didn't forget yours that morning, you are bound to meet someone who did. It's not just your face that will burn, remember your neck, ears, head (if you are lacking hair) and your arms and hands in the spring time. When it is cloudy, don't be fooled into thinking that you don't need sunscreen. Ultra Violet rays will still penetrate the clouds and burn any unprotected skin.

LIP BALM – Protect your lips from the sun, cold and wind with a lip balm with an SPF number of at least 15. Carry a stick of lip balm with you every time you ride. Guaranteed your other half will thank you later!

STOMP PADS – More of a necessity than an accessory, but there are many different types of pads available in various shapes and sizes.

POWER STRAPS – Web strap with velcro closure used around the top of the boot to give added support and stiffness to the boot.

HEEL ANCHORS – Web straps linked together to form a three piece, adjustable accessory that helps to hold your heel back in the boot. These work very well, securing your foot in the boot and providing extra board control as a result.

TOE BLOCKS – If you have large feet and your toes overhang the front of the binding, then you need these. When you put pressure on your overhanging toes, they have to reach the boards top deck before they can exert any pressure on the boards edge. With these rubber blocks, the base of the binding is essentially lengthened increasing toe contact and improving board control.

MINI TOOL – If you only carry one accessory, this is the one. So many times you will be miles from the base lodge and you lose a binding strap. Now what do you do? Struggle down the hill without much control, kicking yourself for not tightening those screws earlier when you noticed that they were loose. Of course, if you had been carrying a mini tool . . .

Back packs and board bags are an essential
part of every snowboarder's kit.
(K2 Snowboards)

BOARD LOCK – It's a sad state of affairs when you can't even leave your snowboard outside a restaurant for ten minutes without it being ripped off. That's one down side of such a popular sport – the crooks out there know that they can sell snowboards instantly because of the huge second hand market. Don't give them the pleasure, carry one of these special light weight cable locks – if you are with buddies, share a lock so you don't all have to carry one.

BACK PACKS – There's one for every occasion, from the small day pack to a full-on hiking pack with special board carrying straps. Remember that a pack will hinder your riding ability to a certain extent, so have a more experienced member of your group carry the pack. It's sometimes a good idea to throw all your group's accessories and spare clothing in one bag and carry it in shifts.

HIP PACK – If the back pack is too big and you don't need to carry that much stuff, then the hip pack could be the answer. There are hundreds of sizes available.

BOARD BAG – Travelling to and from the ski area often means taking different modes of transport. All employees of public transportation companies are trained in the art of spotting your beloved board and making every effort to do as much damage as possible to the edges, base, top sheet – in fact any area of the board that is exposed. So do yourself a favour, be prepared and always use protection. Invest in a fully padded board bag.

Different Disciplines

Which Will You Choose?

Obviously if you have never been on a snowboard before, then you probably will be wondering about the point of this question. The reason is that very soon after that first lesson and first bruised butt (sorry, ego!), you will have passed the stages of basic instruction on rental equipment and will need to purchase some gear of your own. Naturally it helps to know what to buy and in order to do that you need to know what the discipline choices are within the sport of snowboarding.

Of course, there will be a certain percentage of people who will opt for an all round board that will work in all conditions and to a certain degree, perform in each discipline, but others will want to specialise, for example to ride half pipes or to race gates.

What follows is an explanation of each available discipline within snowboarding.

Below: Commercial half pipes need constant maintenance to keep them in the excellent condition of this example at Steamboat Springs, Colorado.

Half pipe

In skateboarding, a half pipe made of plywood is used to keep the riders in perpetual motion and to enable them to jump out and above the 'lip' performing acrobatic 'airs'. As snowboarding has a background in skateboarding and many skaters cross-over to the snow bringing their own tricks with them, so the half pipe has been reproduced in ski areas. half pipes are built down the fall-line, on a slope with a shallow gradient. They are about 100-200 metres in length, vary in width and have a flat

bottom which curves upwards at either wall (the 'transition') ending in a vertical top section. Freestyle competitions revolve around the half pipe and thus there are professional snowboarders that specialise in this discipline.

However, not every ski area has its own half pipe. Pipes need constant maintenance to keep them in good shape and this costs money and know how. So, if you are a budding Terje Hakkonsen and want to ride the pipe constantly, you may have to relocate. Having said that, a half pipe is of course just a series of quarter pipe hits, which can be found all over every ski area in the world, so all is not lost!

As far as the equipment is concerned, a half pipe board, while designed for use in the pipe, is versatile enough to be used as an everyday freestyle board, although it is necessarily short, fat and of a lighter weight which may be restricting to some riders in that it will not suffice in crud, powder or at high speeds. Stance positions will be wide and centred.

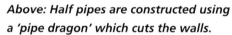

Above: Half pipes are constructed using a 'pipe dragon' which cuts the walls.

Half pipes at Brighton, Utah (left) and Steamboat Springs, Colorado (below).

Freestyle

Even though half pipe riding is classed as a freestyle event, freestyle riding also covers other areas such as flat ground tricks. If you were to class yourself as a freestyler, you would be riding the half pipe on occasion, making use of all the quarter pipes and hits on the ski slopes and performing flat-ground tricks such as ollies, nollies, jibbing, bonking and riding fakie.

A freestyle snowboard is very similar to a half pipe board but in general is slightly longer, marginally narrower with more nose shovel and tail kick. Stance positions are wide to wider and centred on the board.

Freestyle is probably the most popular discipline with new riders, especially those crossing over from skateboarding. It is very dynamic, acrobatic and is responsible for creating many tricks that every new snowboarder aspires to replicate. These are explained later in this book.

The term 'New School' is associated with freestyle. New School is the style of riding that represents the latest and fastest tricks, clothes, haircuts and attitudes. New schoolers are on the cutting edge of freestyle snowboarding, pushing the technicality and imagination of tricks one more step. There is no limit to how far freestyle can be pushed through individual creativity.

Freestyle tricks such as these are very dynamic and call for a high degree of expertise. Freestyle is the most popular discipline for new riders, especially those who cross over from skateboarding.

DIFFERENT DISCIPLINES

Freeriding

As the word suggests, freeriding encompasses all aspects of snowboarding and requires the rider to create their own style and to explore the entire mountain, utilising all the available terrain, both on and off the groomed slopes.

Snowboards designed specifically for freeriding tend to be longer and narrower with more side cut, they have a longer nose shovel and the riders stance is narrower than freestylers' and positioned slightly towards the rear of the board to improve its powder riding characteristics. However, these boards can sometimes be too specific to riding fast in deep powder – by using a longer freestyle board and utilising the many different stance options depending on the snow conditions, a freestyle board will give you the connection between body and earth to ride anywhere at any level.

While many of us would like to be able to perform the highly technical freestyle tricks that even 10 year olds now make look easy, the truth of the matter is that the majority of us are, and will continue to be, freeriders of some description! And we'll be proud of it – freeriding is the pure essence of snowboarding, keeping alive the roots of the sport through the rush and adrenaline pump that comes with high speed cranked turns in bottomless powder under clear blue skies.

Alpine/Racing

Here we move into the field of hard boots and high speed carves on well groomed slopes. Alpine snowboarding is at the very opposite end of the spectrum to half pipe riding – they are essentially two different sports. Race boards were created when racers realised that they were never going to be able to perform technical, high speed slalom turns in soft boots and on the freestyle boards of the time, and since then racing has continued to evolve into the highly technical sport of gate bashing where helmets and body armour go hand in hand with speed suits and the art of mixing waxes for that extra speed.

Snowboard racing is a huge buzz but requires much time training to be able to learn the fastest line down a slalom or giant slalom race course.

For the less ambitious, there are de-tuned race boards available for the alpine free-rider which are wider than technical race boards, have less side cut and are suited to more of the mountain than just the race course. If you are an alpine free-rider, you will find yourself carving powerful turns on the groomed slopes and graceful arcs in the powder – but stay away from the half pipe! Hard boots and a stiff flexing board are not suited to freestyle activities!

Freeriding is the pure essence of snowboarding, allowing the rider to create their own style and to explore the terrain of the entire mountain, not just the highly groomed slopes. It is probably one of the most thrilling and exhilarating disciplines that any snowboarder can enjoy.

Right: Snowboard racing requires a great deal of experience and training to be able to negotiate the fastest line down a slalom race course.

Techniques — How to...

The following instructional section has not been written as the definitive How to snowboard manual. This section should be used to gain valuable information on the techniques of snowboarding and then combined with a lesson with a qualified snowboard instructor. You cannot expect to learn how to snowboard simply by digesting the contents of this book.

THE FIRST DAY

WHICH STANCE? – The very first question that you need to ask yourself is not, What on earth am I doing here?!, but rather, am I goofy or regular? Now, that could be taken personally by some people, but all it means is, which foot is your front foot? The majority of riders (about 70%) are, for some genetic reason, regular foot, and the rest are goofy foot. It makes no difference if you are right or left handed, or which foot you kick with. Regular foot is with the left foot forwards and goofy is with the right.

How do you know which way inclined you are? Well, if you have ever skateboarded, waterskied (single ski) or surfed then you will know, but if not, here are two good tests that you can do in order to determine your particular persuasion.

Imagine that you are back in the school playground and there is ice on the ground. You are sliding around with your friends – you will naturally put one foot in front of the other. Try it in the kitchen on a linoleum floor in your oldest socks! This will show you the way to stand.

Make yourself angry and pretend to shoulder barge into a door. The shoulder that comes out bruised is the same shoulder that you will lead with on your snowboard.

There is no one test that will categorically tell you if you are goofy or regular, but at least they give you an idea and somewhere to begin. Once out on the slopes, if you are uncomfortable with your chosen stance, change it around and try the other way. That is the beauty of snowboarding, it's easy to alter the equipment set-up to suit everybody's ride characteristics.

Stance/Width Angles

Just about all snowboards are made with a pre-set insert pattern, giving the rider a vast amount of stance position choices for width and angles. How should you set up your stance? Well, choosing the right stance is very much a personal decision and takes a few trial runs to figure out what works best for you. Here are a few pointers to put you on the right track:

Freestylers use a wider stance. This is more stable for landing jumps and performing freestyle manoeuvres. A wide stance is 21 inches and above.

Alpine riders use a narrower stance to produce more powerful turns and improve the carving characteristics of the board – the board can be flexed more when pressure is applied to the middle of the board thus giving dynamic turns. A narrow stance is 17 inches and below.

Freestylers use flatter binding angles, ranging from -10° through 0° to around 20° (almost directly across

the board). This, again improves stability and also riding fakie.

Alpine riders use steeper angles (bindings angled towards the nose of the board) to perform dynamic carved turns with more precision. Racers use very steep angles (45° – 60°) while freeriders use lower angles for less aggressive cruising.

Note: The size of your foot will to a certain extent determine the angles available to you. If you have large feet, you will find that your toes and heels will overhang the edges of the board if you try to use flat angles. Thus you need to turn the binding until the overhang is sufficiently reduced.

Binding Positions

Again, with all the available binding positions, you can place your feet anywhere along the length of the board. Huh? Well, you can have the bindings centred on the board (equal distance from either end to each binding) or back off centre. For freestyle, the centred stance works best – riding fakie is easier and again stability is improved. For general freeriding, some prefer to be set back from centre one inch to prevent digging the nose of the board into the snow. For powder riding, being set back off centre is imperative to prevent constant submarine imitations. If your weight is over the rear of the board, the nose will remain out of the powder and the board will float better in deep snow. Experiment with various positions to find your preference.

Foot Centring

Once you have decided on your stance position, you need to position the binding so that your foot is centred across the board. This enables you to exert the maximum pressure on the heel and toe edge and prevents extra toe or heel overhang. Most bindings have foot centring adjustments.

Above left and right: Concentrate on achieving the perfect riding stance.

Basic Riding Stance

Before you ride, you need to know the correct riding stance. This is essential to facilitate a rapid progression through the learning curve. You should concentrate on perfecting the following:

- 80% of your body weight should be over your front foot.
- Bend at your knees, not at the waist. Your knees are your shock absorbers.
- Keep your back straight and vertical.
- Keep your head up, eyes looking ahead and not down at your board.
- Use your arms for balance. To begin with they can be outstretched.
- Stand parallel with the board, then turn your hips, shoulders, and head slightly across the board. (ie facing the direction of travel.)
- Relax! This is the key – being tense will make snowboarding more difficult to learn.

Above: Group stretching before riding.

Stretching

Before you strap in and begin any of the following exercises, it is important to loosen up. Snowboarding is like no other sport or activity that you have ever done and uses muscles that you probably haven't used in a while – you will be surprised how much you use your upper body muscles especially. Your body will be twisting in various directions and you will be exerting all sorts of unfamiliar pressures on yourself. Thus you need to prepare your body for these unfamiliar actions, especially if you are no longer a spring chicken. Don't be fooled by watching young kids head straight for the half pipe and instantly rip it up – when you are young and supple, stretching doesn't seem to be necessary, but it always is. What ever your age, if you warm up and stretch before you ride, you will improve your performance 100%. Plus you stand less of a chance of pulling muscles and having to spend the next day in a hot tub instead of riding that steep, deep, fresh powder. Check out the stretching section on pages 84-87.

Strapping In

Ok, you should now find yourself on the snow, board under arm and heart a'-thumping in anticipation. Strapping into the bindings is the first step in your snowboarding career. Select a flat section of well groomed soft packed snow at the base of the mountain and take a seat. Before you even place your board on the snow, you should be aware that your snowboard can be transformed into a lethal weapon by letting go of it on a slope and seeing it disappear into the distance and carve its way through groups of skiers and snowboarders. To prevent losing your board in this manner, fasten the leash to your front leg before releasing your grasp on the board. The next step is to buckle your front foot into the front binding. Remember to clear any snow or ice from the underside of your boots and from inside the binding before trying to strap in. When fastening the buckles, begin with the ankle strap,

Strapping into the bindings.

then the toe strap and finally the top strap (if applicable). If you are using plate (hard) bindings, follow the same sequence but obviously attach the binding depending on whether it has a toe clip or heel clip. Toe clips are the most common and most effective – insert the heel under the rear bail then fasten the toe clip. If heel clips are used, simple reverse the process. Ok, later on you will use the same method to buckle your back foot at this stage and be ready to ride, but for now leave the back foot out and let's go through some basic exercises.

How to Fall

As a beginner, you WILL fall and fall often! Be prepared for a few bruises and aching muscles. The injuries associated with snowboarding are different from those common in skiing. Skiers tend to suffer more from twisting their knees, whereas the more popular snowboard injuries are damaged wrists and bruised butts and knees. Snowboarders do not twist their knees as much as skiers but do land on them a lot at first. The worst falls come from catching an edge. So, learning how to fall will help prevent the worst injuries.

When falling forwards, do not use your hands to stop yourself. Either clench your fists and land on them or try to land on your forearms. Wrists break and sprain easily. Repeatedly landing on your knees can be painful – wear skateboard type knee pads to protect the knees. These can be worn underneath baggy pants. Also a lot of snowboard pants come with extra built in padding in the necessary areas.

When falling backwards, there is not much that you can do except land on your butt. However, do try to relax. If you fall and tense up (which is the

Fasten the leash to your front leg.

Learn how to fall correctly, to avoid injury.

Above: With your front foot in the binding, use your other foot to push the board in a straight line.

natural reaction), you can do more damage, possibly to your back and neck, than if you are relaxed. When tense you are more likely to miss your butt altogether and land on your head, which in most cases is not as well protected! A tip for beginners is to shove some kind of cushioning material down your pants to protect your butt. You may receive some strange looks but at least you'll be able to sit down later in the bar!

Later, when you fall on a steeper slope, you need to regain control before you start to slide uncontrollably down the slope. If you find yourself in a prone position, facing either head first or feet first down the hill, dig the edge of the board into the snow as soon as possible in order to slow yourself down to a stop.

Balance Exercises

Note 1: Toe edge   The edge of the board under your toes.

Heel edge – The edge of the board under your heels.

Note 2: All of the following beginner exercises require the rider to be able to move and flex without restriction. The use of soft boots and soft bindings is therefore recommended. Hard boots, especially ski boots do not possess the necessary flex characteristics to allow the full range of movement essential to the beginner.

To become more familiar with the sensation of riding a snowboard, try the following exercises:

With the front foot only in the binding, choose a flat section of snow and skate yourself around as you would on a skateboard. When you are moving, place your pushing foot on the stomp pad between the bindings. You should be able to grasp the general feeling of riding a snowboard with this exercise. This is also the method that you will use to move around on flat ground and when getting on and off lifts.

Right: As you become more confident, skate the board on a flat area of snow, increasing the duration of each glide.

Walk up a slope by digging the toe edge of the board into the snow directly across the fall-line.

Next find a very slight slope, preferably one that ends in a flat or uphill area. Stand with the board facing down the slope, again with just the front foot attached. Now push off with the other foot as before and place the foot on the stomp pad. Remember to lean forward, keeping your weight over your front knee. Because of the slope, you should be able glide for a distance before coming to rest on the flat section. Try this a few times, concentrating on your correct basic riding stance. When returning to the top of the slope again, it is not necessary to remove the board from your foot – you can walk up the slope by digging the toe edge of the board into the snow directly across the fall-line.

The next step is to initiate a turn, still with only the front foot in the binding. As you pick up speed at the bottom of the slope, try a toeside turn, ie turn to the left if goofy and to the right if regular. The turn is initiated with your upper body while applying pressure to your toe edge and lifting your heels. To begin the turning motion, turn your head back up the hill while moving your shoulders, hips and arms in the same direction. If you keep your weight over the front foot, the

board will be forced to turn because of your upper body movement. At this stage you do not have much momentum so do not expect to turn too rapidly. In fact, you will notice that by making the turn, you actually bring the board to a stop. The art of stopping incorporates the same body and board movements as turning. Later on we will cover turning and stopping in more depth and at higher speeds. This exercise is just to develop the basic concept of turning.

Next try turning the opposite direction, ie a heelside turn. Most beginners find this turn more difficult

Try a toeside turn with the front foot in the binding. Turn to the right if regular, or to the left if you are goofy.

than the toeside turn. As before, push off down a slight slope and glide. As you reach the bottom of the slope, keep your weight over your front foot and turn your upper body in the direction that you want to go. You can also use your arms to point in the direction of travel which will help the board to turn. By turning the board in this manner, you will bring the board to a stop.

While you still have just the front foot connected to the board, you should become familiar with some of the other movements that are necessary for snowboarding:-

Try walking the board in a turn, in both directions.

Turn in the other direction – heelside.

Walk the board in a turn in one direction, then change direction to become familiar with both movements.

Stand with the free foot on the stomp pad on a level section of snow, then put alternate pressure on the toes and on the heels, as you would in a turn situation. Notice that too much angulation will result in an unstable position. In other words you will fall over! Note: Greater angulation is necessary at higher speeds.

With your free foot on the stomp pad, put alternate pressure on your toes (below) and on your heels (right).

Balance Exercises – Both Feet Strapped

Still on the flat area of snow, strap your rear foot into the binding and stand up. To become familiar with having both feet strapped in and to test the limits of the snowboard, try the following exercises.

Jump up and down, landing flat on the base of the board, cushioning the landing by flexing at the knees.

Jump up and turn the board 90° in either direction. Use your upper body to

Jump up and down, cushioning the landing by flexing at your knees.

help spin the board but try not to counter rotate the body once the turn is completed (ie do not rotate your body back again.)

Explore the forward and backward flexing limits of your snowboard. Lean your weight all the way back and all the way forward, trying to balance on the tail and then the nose of the board. Sometimes you will find yourself in these weird positions after landing a jump for instance and it is good for your sanity to know that you can retain control of your board from such extremes and return to a normal riding stance.

Above: Jump up and turn your board 90° in either direction, using your upper body to help you spin the board.

Explore the forward (left) and backward (below) flexing limits of your board. This is good practice for retaining your balance when landing after a jump.

Stopping

From this point on, you will be carrying out exercises with both of your feet strapped to the board. You need to know how to stop! The art of stopping involves the use of your edges to control the boards motion. The following exercises are designed to allow you to explore various movements of the snowboard while controlling the board by using different edge angulation. When you apply pressure to one of the edges and lift the other edge off the snow, the edge that is in contact with the snow will have greater angulation, thus creating greater friction and the board will be forced to turn and/or slow down. side slipping, traversing, garlands and the falling leaf exercise all improve your edge and board control, making speed reduction and stopping easier and more efficient.

Side Slipping

There will be many occasions during your snowboarding life that you need to use the board's edge; first and foremost to stop and later to control yourself at high speeds or on steep slopes.

It is essential that one of the first skills you learn is the ability to side slip. Using the same gentle gradient as before, hike up to the top, sit facing down the slope and strap your back foot into the board as well as the front. Standing up from this position is not easy, so roll over so that you are now kneeling and facing up the slope with your board across the fall-line. Now you can stand up onto your toe edge. It is essential to relax and to keep equal weight over both feet. Use your arms for balance, face your upper body directly up the hill and gradually reduce the amount of edge angulation. More edge

Roll over so you are facing up the slope.

Now stand up, on to your toeside edge.

angle creates more friction and thus less movement (you stop!). As you reduce the angle of the edge by lowering the heels to the snow, the board will begin to slide. Control your speed by applying pressure to the toeside edge and lifting your heels. If you don't fall in this exercise then you are very talented!

Side slipping down the fall-line is very difficult to master at first.

Once you have become proficient at side slipping on the toes, you should try side slipping on the heel edge. Begin by sitting facing down the slope with your heel edge across the fall-line. Standing up from this position is not easy, especially on a slope. The best way is to reach out with the front arm while pushing up from behind you with the other arm. You will begin to slide as you stand up so keep your weight equally over both feet and control your speed with the angulation of the heel edge. To slow down apply pressure to the heel edge and lift the toes.

When trying these side slipping exercises, remember to stand upright with a slight flex in the knees and with your head up, not looking at your board.

You must maintain equal weight over both feet during a side slip otherwise the board will begin to move across the slope instead of down the fall-line. If you feel the nose of the board begin to slide down the fall-line then you have too much pressure on the front foot. Counteract this movement by moving your weight back over the rear foot until the board resumes its side slipping position, directly across the fall-line, and you have equal weight over both feet again. If you feel the tail of the board begin to slide down the fall-line, then you have put too much pressure on the back foot. Move your weight over the front foot until you resume the side slipping position.

During your first lesson on the hill, your instructor may well help you in this side slipping exercise by supporting you by holding your hands, thus helping you to balance at first.

Warning!

During both of these exercises and over the next few sessions, you will discover the phenomenon of 'catching an edge'! As yet, you have not been moving at any real speed and falling should not yet hurt, but imagine face planting at 30mph! This is quite common and is

Side slipping, toeside. Lower your heels to the snow and the board will start to slide.

Stand up from the heelside of your board. You will begin to slide as you stand up.

normally due to catching an edge. In these early side slipping exercises, be aware that if you do not have much edge angulation and the board becomes flat on the snow, that the downhill edge will dig into the snow and flip you over, either onto your face or onto your butt. Neither is preferable and both can be painful and result in injury. So be aware at all times of catching edges.

Side slipping on the heelside edge. Keep your weight equally spread over both feet and control your speed by adjusting the pressure on the heel edge of your board.

Skidded Transverses

When you can side slip both heelside and toeside in a proficient manner, next you should try a side slip with a traversing action. Once you have momentum in the side slipping stance, simply move your body weight over your front foot so that you are exerting more pressure on your front foot than on your back foot. Immediately, the nose of your board will begin to move across the fall-line into a traverse. If you were to maintain the pressure on your front foot, the board would keep turning until it was facing directly down the fall-line. This is the next step when we learn how to turn. For now, however, once your weight has shifted enough to make the board traverse across the slope, transfer some of the weight back onto the rear foot to hold the traverse in that plane. Moving your weight back so that you have equal weight over both feet again will take you back to the side slipping position. As you experiment, you will find that you can traverse equally as well by applying pressure to your rear foot thus traversing fakie (backwards) across the slope. Remember to turn your upper body slightly to face the direction of travel as you slide in a fakie traverse. Try the same exercise on both the heel and toe edges.

Skidded transverse – heelside, forward.

Skidded transverse – heelside, fakie.

Skidded transverse – toeside, forward.

Skidded transverse – toeside, fakie.

Falling Leaf Exercise

In this exercise, you will create a movement similar to that of a leaf falling from a tree. Follow the same movements as if you were about to traverse across the slope. This time, as the nose of the board moves down the fall-line, transfer all your weight to your back foot so that the rear of the board begins to move down the slope. Immediately transfer the weight back to the front foot again etc. Don't you just feel like a falling leaf?! This exercise is very true to life in that you will use this method of side slipping to negotiate difficult terrain such as rocky outcrops or groups of people in crowded areas. Try this on both your heel and toe edges. Remember to turn your upper body in the direction of travel.

Falling leaf exercise – toeside.

Garlands

A Garland is basically half of a turn. In this exercise you will learn to link a series of garlands together in order to experience the sensation of beginning a turn without having to point the board directly down the hill. Becoming proficient at this exercise will build up your confidence for the completed turn and will teach you how to control the speed of your board culminating in a complete stop.

From a side slipping position on your toe edge, shift 80% of your weight over your front foot and turn your upper body towards the nose of the board. As the nose of the board begins to slide down the fall-line, lower your

centre of gravity by flexing at the knees. This helps you to exert pressure on the toe edge thus remaining in control of your board. Then turn your upper body back up the hill while sliding the back foot down the hill with pressure on the toes. Lift the heels up to give greater edge angulation and the board will return to a side slipping position. As you bring the board back across the fall-line, stand up slightly to un-weight the board in preparation for the next half-turn. Repeat the exercise, linking the half-turns together. It is not necessary to come to a complete stop every time you bring the board perpendicular to the fall-line.

Next try to perform garlands on the heel edge. From a side slipping position

on the heel edge, shift 80% of your weight over the front foot, keeping your upper body facing down the slope. As the nose of the board begins to slide down the fall-line, lower your centre of gravity by flexing at the knees. This helps you to exert pressure on the heel edge thus remaining in control of your board. Keeping your weight over your front foot, turn your upper body in the direction of intended travel while sliding your back foot down the hill with pressure on the heel edge. Lift the toes to give greater heel edge angulation and the board will return to a side slipping position. Start all over and link the half turns together to form heelside garlands.

Below: A garland is basically half a turn.

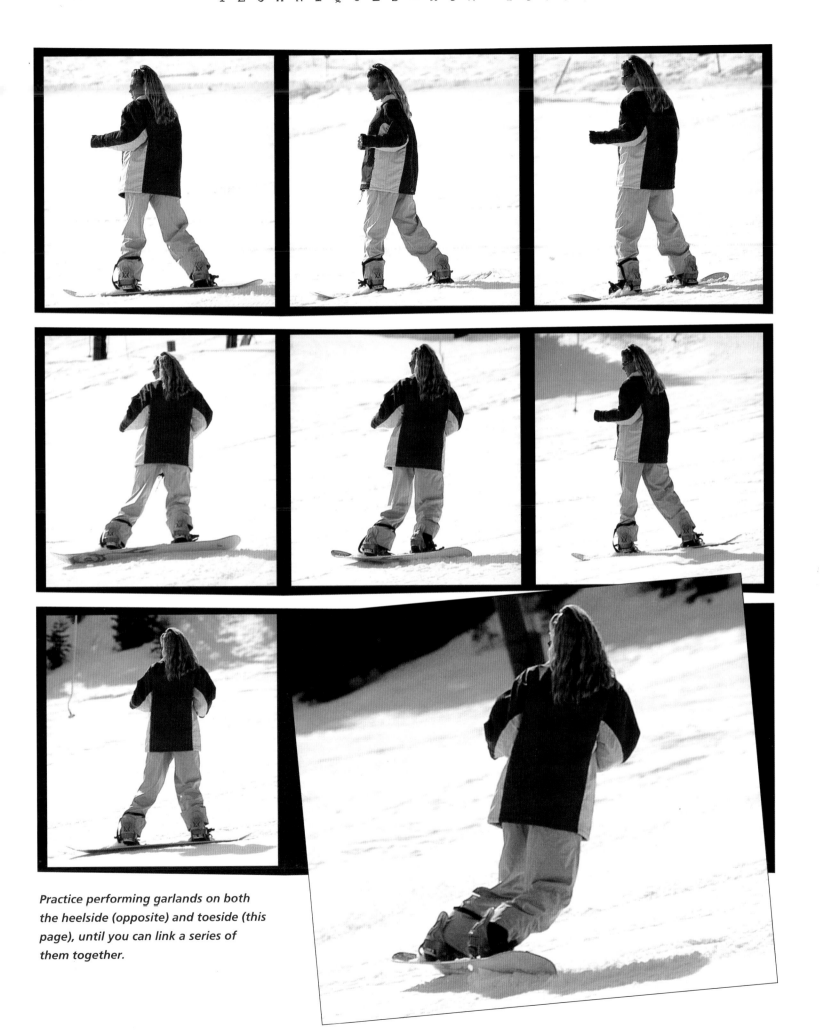

Practice performing garlands on both the heelside (opposite) and toeside (this page), until you can link a series of them together.

Riding the Lifts

By now you are probably wondering how much more hiking you have to do! It's tiring isn't it? Don't worry, now it's time to make use of those drag lifts and chair lifts. In some ski resorts, the lifts on the nursery (beginner) slopes at the base of the mountain may be free. So you don't have to buy a ski pass for another day or so.

The Drag Lift

These lifts come in various shapes and sizes, with rope tows, T-Bars and button lifts being the most common.

All the earlier exercises that you practiced with just the front foot in the binding will show their worth now. Whenever you ride such a lift, always remove the rear foot from the binding. Once in position to receive the rope, bar or button, stand with the rear foot on the snow to steady yourself. Flex at the knees and remain relaxed. Take hold of the rope with both hands. Place the T-bar behind you and sit on it. Put the button between your legs. In all cases,

lean back slightly and anticipate the initial pull of the lift. If you lean over the front of the board too much, the lift will pull you off balance and dump you on the snow in front of all those laughing skiers. As soon as you receive the bar or button, place your rear foot on the stomp pad between the bindings. It is very important to keep your snowboard flat on the snow and pointing directly up the slope (ie in the direction of travel.) As soon as you put the board up on an edge or turn across the lift track, it is almost guaranteed that you will fall. And there is nothing worse than being dragged on your back up a drag lift. If you relax, keep the board flat and lean back slightly keeping your weight over the rear of the board, you'll be at the top before you know it.

Unloading

Suddenly you are at the top of the lift – what next? First you need to pull down on the button or bar, in order to release it from your person. Sometimes you can catch the end of the T-bar in your

jacket as you are unloading – not a good idea! So be sure to check that you are separated from the lift before letting go and gliding off into the unloading area. Well, remember all those one footed sliding exercises that we did? This is where you need them. Keeping your rear foot on the stomp pad, assume the basic riding position (transfer your weight forward again), knees bent, head up, arms out for balance, relax and slide off into the unloading area. At the top of most lifts, the exit area will be flat with an upgrade to slow you down – you will come to a natural stop. Some lifts may have a steep off ramp, but if you are using a beginner lift for your first run, the ski area has been kind enough to build a fail-safe natural stopping area. They have seen your type before!

Something to watch out for – more often than not, there will be groups of people just standing around either discussing the weather or poring over maps – whatever they are doing, you are heading right for them and someone is about to lose their legs! So, look ahead as you unload from the lift and steer into a clear area if necessary. You already know how to make a directional change with only one foot in. If unsure, perform a side slip to a stop. If desperate, sit down and you will stop immediately! This may not be the most glamourous of entrances into the snowboarding world, but it has happened to us all at one time or another.

If you do fall, pick yourself up quickly and move out of the way of the next lift full of uncontrollables.

Regardless, always move away from the unloading area as quickly as possible to avoid congestion, and find a safe place to strap-in.

Left: This group of young snowboarders show the correct way to unload.

The correct way to get on to a moving chair lift. As you sit on the chair, lift the tip of your board and keep it pointed straight ahead.

As you unload from the lift, make sure that none of your clothing is caught in the chair and that your bindings are fastened.

The Chair Lift

Note: At first you may need to carry your board up on the chair – so make sure this is allowed at your ski area.

Use your skating skills to position yourself in the lift line and to negotiate the maze. As the chair in front of you passes the loading entrance, move into the loading area quickly and stand with your rear foot on the snow to steady yourself. Look over your shoulder to anticipate the oncoming chair. As you sit down on the chair, lift up the tip of your board as well as keeping it straight and pointed in the direction of travel. If you twist it at all, you are going to catch an edge and find that your legs become contorted and jammed between the chair and the snow. If the chair has foot rests, use them to rest your legs from the weight of the board. If not, rest the board on the toe of your free (back) foot.

Unloading

As you approach the off ramp at the top of the lift, you should prepare to unload. Make sure that none of your clothing is caught in the chair and that your bindings are fastened (sometimes you will loosen them on the chairlift to release any pressure). As you near the ramp, lift up the nose of the board to prevent it from catching. Once the board is in contact with the snow, keep it flat and pointing straight down the slope of the off ramp. Place your hands on the front edge of the chair and push gently off with your rear foot on the stomp pad. Do not try to put your free foot down on the snow first as it will act as a brake and you'll be down! Always go with the slope and don't try to fight gravity. As you glide away, assume the basic stance position, keep your weight forward and slide into the unloading area as explained for the drag lifts. Remember, if you lean back the board will slide out from under you and you will feel like you just stepped on a banana peel! If this happens, jump to your feet as soon as possible and push yourself out of the way of the next chair full of potential disasters!

Riding a chair, with boards attached.

BASIC SLIDE TURNS

Performing a basic slide turn requires you to combine all the skills that have been learned thus far. The first turns that you will learn will essentially be linked traverses. As you will be making wide turns across the slope, it is important that you take time to choose an area of snow that is not congested. As you make each turn, be sure to watch for other skiers and snowboarders approaching – be ready to abort the turn at any given moment and assume the side slipping stance.

Key Points to Turning

Remember the basic riding stance at all times.

- Head up, arms out for balance.
- Your head, shoulders, arms and hips move in the direction of the turn.
- Keep knees bent and flexible at all times.
- Have 80% of your weight over the front foot as you turn.
- Extend your body upwards between turns to release edge pressure thus helping the edge change.

The Toeside Turn

Begin from the side slipping position on the heelside edge, weight evenly distributed on both feet, sliding down the fall-line. This is the same position that you started the garlands exercise from.

Transfer 80% of your weight to the front leg, putting pressure on the front foot.

The nose of the board will naturally begin to turn down the fall-line. As it does, maintain weight over the front foot and allow the board to leave the heel edge and glide on the base for an instant.

Once the board is gliding down the fall-line on its base, transfer pressure to the toe-edge while maintaining weight on the front foot. At this stage it is imperative that you do not lean back. Moving your weight to the rear of the board, over the back foot, at this point, will make turning very difficult if not impossible. In fact, you will simply pick up speed directly down the fall-line and will quickly find yourself totally out of control.

As you begin to pressure the toe edge, you should use your upper body to aid the turning process. Pick a spot further up the slope from where you are and turn your head, arms, shoulders and hips towards the chosen point. Do not swing the body, simply turn and hold in that position until the board follows. At the same time, slide the rear foot down the slope on the toe edge.

Once you have completed the turn, you will find yourself in the familiar toe edge side slipping position. At this point, it is important to keep your weight on the front foot until the turn is completed otherwise weight will be transferred to the back foot and you will begin to slide backwards across the fall-line. You learned how to control this movement in the initial exercises.

The toeside turn.

The Heelside Turn

Begin from the side slipping position on the toeside edge, weight evenly distributed over both feet, moving down the fall-line. Concentrate on a correct riding stance.

Transfer 80% of your weight to the front leg, putting pressure on the front foot.

The nose of the board will naturally begin to turn down the fall-line. As it does, maintain weight over the front foot and allow the board to leave the toe edge and glide on the base for an instant.

Once the board is gliding down the fall-line on its base, transfer pressure to the heel edge and lift up your toes while maintaining 80% of your weight on the front foot. At this stage it is imperative that you do not lean back. Moving your weight towards the rear of the board, over the rear foot, at this point, will make turning very difficult, if not impossible. In fact, you will simply pick up speed directly down the fall-line and will quickly find yourself totally out of control.

As you begin to pressure the heel edge, you should use your upper body to aid the turning process. Turn your upper body towards the direction of intended travel, pointing your arms and looking at where you want to go. At the same time, slide your back foot down the hill.

The heelside turn is more difficult than the toeside turn and you will need to commit yourself to make the turn because you are forcing your body into an un-natural position. Don't worry, it will become very natural! Remember, do not swing the upper body.

Once you have completed the turn, you will find yourself back in the heelside side slipping position (ie the beginning of the toeside turn). This completes the heelside turn.

The heelside turn.

Linking Turns

Now that you can perform both the basic heelside and toeside turns individually, the next stage is to link the two turns together, thus making linked basic turns. At this time you should begin to add another motion to the process.

As you begin to make each turn from the side slipping position, lower your centre of gravity by flexing at the knees (not at the waist – keep your back upright). This is called down-weighting and adds more power to the turn by making the edge grip more effectively on the snow. At the completion of each turn, you need to counteract this motion by standing up slightly (up-weighting) and releasing the pressure from the active edge thus reducing its grip on the snow and making it easier to turn to the other edge.

At this stage, concentrate on reducing the length of time that you spend on the traverse between turns. This will increase the speed of your turns and decrease the number of times that you obstruct other snowboarders and skiers!

Warning

When changing edges during the turn at this stage, it is important not to attempt to change too soon. The board must be pointing directly down the fall-line and the base of the board should be flat with neither edge in contact with the snow, before you change to the next edge. If you attempt to change too soon, you will catch the wrong edge and will be flipped onto either your face or your butt.

NOTE 1: Do not try to perform the turn by swinging the upper body in the direction of the turn. This is a common mistake which, if repeated, can become a bad habit. This is known as counter rotation and throws the body out of balance, the result being incorrect turning at a later stage, making carving, especially on the heelside turn, impossible to perfect.

NOTE 2: Remember that once the board is pointed down the fall-line it will accelerate. Do not panic! The natural reaction is to lean back. Resist

this temptation and maintain the weight on the front foot to carry you through the turn.

NOTE 3: Now that you can perform the basic slide turns on both the heelside and toeside edge and can link them together with confidence, you are ready to progress to the intermediate stage.

Once you can perform both heelside and toeside turns, you can link them together.

INTERMEDIATE TURNS

The goals at this stage are as follows:

- To reduce the length of time that you are in the traversing position between turns.
- To perform more flowing movements and thus more rhythmic turns.
- To decrease the radius of the turns.
- To increase the speed of travel.
- To begin the progression to carved turns.

By now you will have been snowboarding for a few days and feel confident that you are ready to pick up the pace a little. So let's go!

It's time to lose the training wheels and add some intermediate techniques. At the beginner stage, you were taught certain movements in order to help you through the early stages. Once you have mastered the basic turning techniques, these are no longer necessary.

Key Points:

- Start to turn the upper body less when initiating the turn.
- Concentrate on using the hips and shoulders as your steering wheel, pointing your leading shoulder in the direction that you want to go.
- You no longer need to slide the back foot down the hill to help the turn.
- The arms no longer need to be extended forwards for balance purposes.
- There should be dynamic body movements in the horizontal and vertical plane, in the form of vertical up and down-weighting and horizontal forward and backward weight transfer.

Learn to develop a confident turning technique as your riding improves

LINKED INTERMEDIATE TURNS

Begin from the side slipping position on the heelside edge. Transfer 80% of your weight on to your front foot as in the basic turns.

As the board starts to turn down the fall-line, begin to down-weight by flexing at the knees.

Allow the nose of the board to turn down the fall-line until the base of the board is flat on the snow and you are off the heel edge.

Allow the board to pick up a little more speed than the basic turn and then begin to pressure your toes and lift up your heels while continuing to down-weight.

At the same time, turn your hips and shoulders slightly to point in the direction that you want to go. The board will turn without the need to slide the back foot down the hill.

Once you have crossed the fall-line and completed the toeside turn you will find yourself in a traversing position on the toe edge.

At this point you need to un-weight the board in order to reduce the pressure on the toe edge while turning your hips and shoulders down the hill slightly in the direction that you want to turn. This initiates the heelside turn.

Remember to have 80% of your weight over your front foot and the nose of the board will naturally move down the fall-line.

As the board starts to turn down the fall-line, begin to down-weight by flexing at the knees.

Allow the nose of the board to turn down the fall-line until the base of the board is flat on the snow and you are off the toe edge. As the board picks up speed, begin to pressure the heel edge, lift up your toes and continue to down weight.

At this stage, the combination of turning your hips and shoulders to point in the direction of intended travel and the exertion of pressure on the edge creates the intermediate turn. Now you should be making medium radius turns in order to keep your speed up. It is easier to perform intermediate turns once you are moving more quickly.

Sequence to demonstrate linked intermediate turns.

CARVING

There is nothing like the feeling that you will experience when you begin to carve. Carving allows you to enter a whole new world of snowboarding. Once you have perfected the intermediate turn in both directions and can link them together, you are ready for some advanced riding. That comes in the form of the carved turn – the most efficient and exhilarating way to make turns down the mountain.

What is Carving?

Carving is an extension of the intermediate turn whereby the board does not slide at all during the turn but instead remains on its edge the whole time, leaving a razor sharp track in the snow.

How Does a Board Carve?

Every board has a specific flex, sidecut and camber which determines its carving capabilities. When pressure is applied to the edge of the board, it bends, creating an opposite camber and forming a curve in the edge which is unique to each board. When this edge is in contact with the snow and a carve turn is performed, the board will turn along the radius of this curve. This is called the turning radius which is created by the side cut – boards are designed with different side cut radii depending on their intended use.

What You Will Need

To execute a carved turn the following criteria are required:
- Hard packed snow
- A slope with a good gradient to build up speed
- Confidence!

The Carved Turn

Build up speed on a toeside traverse in preparation for the heelside turn.

Transfer your weight over the front foot and turn your leading shoulder, hip and eyes to point in the direction that you want to turn. This will initiate the turn.

Begin to down-weight by flexing at the knees and move your hips over the heelside edge. This exerts pressure on the heelside edge and the board will automatically change from the toeside edge to the heelside edge.

Below: This picture shows a toeside carve on a gentle slope.

NOTE: The board is never flat on the snow. Instead, you change from edge to edge instantly during the carve turn. You actually change edges before the board has moved down the fall-line and are momentarily on the wrong edge. Don't panic – as long as you have sufficient speed, the forces that you are exerting on the board will enable you to produce perfect tracks.

Continue to down-weight and pressure the heel edge while pointing your leading shoulder, hip and eyes where you want to go.

As you near the end of the turn, transfer some of your weight back over the rear foot while pushing through the back foot. This will flex the tail of the board producing a tighter curve in the boards edge, creating the sharpest turn radius. This enables you to finish the turn correctly.

As the heelside turn ends, up-weight by flexing upwards slightly at the knees while turning your leading shoulder, hip and eyes towards the new direction of travel.

Transfer your weight to your front foot while moving your knees over the toeside edge. The board will change from the heelside to the toeside edge.

Down-weight through the turn by

This heelside carve demonstrates how the snowboard remains on its edge, sharply cutting in to the snow.

flexing at the knees. Push your knees towards the snow to maintain pressure on the edge and continue to point your leading shoulder, hip and eyes where you want to go.

Finish the turn by transferring some of your weight towards over the back foot and flexing the tail by pushing through the back foot.

Up-weight by flexing at the knees and you are back at stage one, ready for the next heelside turn.

Tips To Help You Carve

Keep your knees apart when turning. In the past, especially with a hard boot/board set-up, it was thought that the back knee should be tucked behind the front knee for optimum performance. Try to push the back knee out perpendicular to the board, and down towards the snow on a toeside turn. On a heelside turn, point your front knee in the direction that you want to go.

You may have to reduce the angle of your bindings if you are using plates. If you have very steeply angled bindings you will find it harder to exert maximum pressure on the boards edge. Flatter binding angles enable you to stand more parallel to the board from where you can easily apply pressure to your toes and heels.

Keep your centre of gravity low by flexing at the knees and not at the waist. Try to keep your upper body as upright as possible. As soon as you begin to lean out away from the board, so your centre of gravity moves out making it more difficult to keep pressure on the edge of the board therefore reducing your board control. You will find that if you lean all the way out into what is known as a Eurocarve, the board will lose its grip on the snow and slide out. It's fun to Eurocarve now and then but don't be surprised if you keep losing it! The Eurocarve is also known as the Vitelli Turn, named after the French perfecter of the move, Serge Vitelli.

The more edge angle that you have the more that the edge can grip the snow when pressurized. So crank the board over onto its edge as far as you can and let the carving begin. If you are using soft boots, watch out for your toes and heels overhanging and catching in the snow when cranking the board up on an edge. You can reduce this by angling the bindings

The Vitelli Turn, named after Serge Vitelli.

further forward or by a simple operation to remove your toes!

If you really want to carve to the limit, you will need a race board with hard boots and bindings. Of course you can carve on a freestyle board with soft boots but if you don't try a race board you will never know the purest feeling of carving.

Check your tracks to see where you are going wrong. You will be able to see if you were sliding out at all on any of the turns and can take steps to make sure that next time you leave a narrow rut that looks like some one just took a razor to the slope.

And Then . . .

Practice, practice, practice. And take an advanced lesson at your local ski area's snowboard school.

Riding Fakie

Probably the first skill you need to learn if you want to ride freestyle. Also known as switch-stance, riding fakie is the art of riding your snowboard backwards with as much ease as when you are riding forwards. If you watch the pros at work you will find it almost impossible to determine if they are naturally goofy or regular because they look so relaxed riding in both directions. Being able to ride fakie will help you enormously when learning freestyle tricks as you will be able to land and take off switch-stance, whether you meant to or not!

So how do you do it? Well, the easiest way is to return to that gentle slope that you were learning on originally and go back to basics. Return to the basic slide turns section of this book and start again. Fakie.

Tips

It will be easier to learn if your bindings are mounted fairly flat across the board. The back foot should be almost at 0°.

Because your front binding, at least, is angled forward you will find it difficult to turn your hips towards the tail of the board. So concentrate on turning your shoulders and head to face rearwards and in the direction that you want to go.

Once you are more familiar with the sensation of riding fakie, try to turn your hips towards the back of the board in order to help the turn. At first they simply will not want to move in this unaccustomed direction but relax and concentrate! Reducing the angle of the front foot will help your fakie riding.

For optimum freestyle and fakie riding, experiment with the angles of both bindings – if you can take a mini tool up on to the hill with you every time you ride you'll be able to make any necessary adjustments on the spot.

Also known as switch-stance, riding fakie is the art of riding your snowboard backwards – essential if you want to ride freestyle.

Ollieing

The ollie comes from the skateboard world and was invented by a skateboarder, Alan Gelfand. It was devised as a way of propelling a skater into the air in order to perform skate tricks. The ollie was transferred to the snowboard world by skaters and has become an extremely important part of freestyle snowboarding. Being able to ollie will give you extra height on a jump and will allow you perfect various flat-ground tricks.

To practice the ollie find a gentle slope with some flat hard packed snow. You don't need too much speed at first and should begin without trying to jump an obstacle. Once you can ollie at low speeds then you can introduce an obstacle to clear and extra speed.

Pick a mark in the snow as an imaginary obstacle. Ride directly down the fall-line towards this point and put the board flat on its base.

As you approach the mark down-weight by flexing at the knees. Keep your back and head upright, eyes looking ahead. Try to lower your centre of gravity as much as possible.

As you hit the take off mark, you need to launch your body upwards while leaning back slightly. At the same time lift the nose of the board off the ground by pulling your front foot and knee upwards while pushing through the back foot to flex the tail of the board.

The flex of the tail will help to spring you into the air as you release the pressure on your back foot. Lift your back foot and knee upwards and you will find yourself soaring gracefully over the earth. Well maybe not quite as dramatically as all that, but you should be a couple of feet off the snow!

Pull your knees up towards your chest and keep your arms out for balance. Try to keep the board directly

Above: Sequence to demonstrate how to ollie.

underneath you and in a horizontal position, ready for the landing.

It is important to spot your landing. Look at where you are going to land and anticipate the impact by extending your legs.

When the board hits the snow, absorb the landing by flexing downwards at the knees. Keep your weight slightly back off the centre of the board. If your weight is too far forwards you will pitch over the front of the board and face plant. It is important to land with the base of the board flat to reduce your chances of catching an edge.

Now find a small obstacle to jump over. As you learn to ollie higher, so you can increase the height of the obstacle. Ollieing is also very useful when jumping as it helps you to gain extra height when launching off a hit. It can also be combined with rotations to perform flat ground tricks.

Sequence to show how to nollie.

Hitting Jumps

Once you can ollie and you have tasted the weightless feeling of being in the air, you will doubtless want to go bigger! The best snow condition in which to practice your first jump is powder or at least soft snow. Why? Because you are going to slam hard during those initial attempts at flying, and a soft landing will extend your life long enough so you can make it home to your real job!

Firstly you need to find a suitable jump. Don't go too big at first, all you need is a small bump on the ski slope to propel yourself skywards.

There are certain criteria to look for in a jump:

Check the take off. There needs to be a smooth run up with only a little kicker. A steep kicker on the take -off will give you more vertical motion than you can handle at this stage.

If the run up is on a traverse across the fall-line, you will find it easier to make the jump from your toeside edge. Thus a jump from a heelside traverse is not the best starting point. It is simply easier to launch from the toeside edge.

Ideally you should be able to approach the jump by riding directly down the fall-line. Then you can take off with the board flat on the snow, as you did when learning how to ollie.

Landing

The bigger the air the more important it is to absorb the impact on landing. As with the ollie this is achieved by flexing at the knees as the board hits the snow. Remember to keep your weight slightly back off centre.

Opposite: Once you can jump and land safely, you can progress to air tricks.

As you get more confident, you will be able to progress to larger jumps.

As you land, flex at the knees to absorb the impact.

Freestyle tricks

Once you are up in the air, what next? There are a number of recognized tricks that you can perform or use as a basis for forming your own versions. Here are a few of the most popular tricks.

Flat Ground Tricks

You don't have to be in the air to perform an impressive trick. There are several that can be done on the flat snow without any bumps or jumps to hit.

And when you can do all these tricks competently, try doing them all switch stance! Once you are at this stage you should wake up one day to find an array of sponsors breaking down your door!

Above: Indy air.   *Below: Lien air.*

Backside 540 Mute.

Frontside 360.

Backside 540 Corkscrew.

Satan Flip (Backflip).

Impressive freestyle tricks require a great deal of expertise and lots of practice to perform skillfully. Here are a few of the better known examples – Invert (opposite, top left); Melancholy (opposite, top right); Mute air (opposite, bottom left); Tail grab (opposite, bottom right); Stalefish (right) and Method (below).

Riding powder

If you have never experienced the adrenaline rush from riding in steep and deep powder, you are in for an incredible shock and had better start praying for snow. This is what snowboarding is all about. Powder makes snowboarding unbelievably easy, no edges to catch, you seem to float effortlessly, pulled by the natural force of gravity.

There is another side to the coin. Powder can be very dangerous in that you can drown if you bail head first into deep snow. Tree wells are a particularly dangerous hazard. Always ride with others and don't leave your buddies behind – wait periodically to re-group. There is a saying among hardened snowboarders – 'There are no friends on powder days'. This could not be further from the truth.

Although there are no edges to catch, there is an equally painful risk. Commonly known as going over the handlebars, digging the nose of the board into the snow brings your run to an abrupt halt. When riding in powder you need to shift your weight back over your rear foot to sink the tail of the board and bring the nose of the board out of the snow. This is much the same as the technique used in surfing. In fact snowboarding in powder gives you much the same feeling as surfing – there are natural windlips out there that resemble endless waves. The mountain itself has been described as the endless wave and a long powder run certainly gives one the same buzz as surfing does.

Another tip for transferring your weight to the rear of the board is to move your bindings back on the board. If they are centred, move them both back about an inch. If they are already set back off centre then you are stoked. If you have a choice of boards, pick the longer one. The more length, the more floatation and the more exhilarating the ride.

There is another expression heard frequently in snowboard circles; 'Speed is your friend'. Don't fight it. It is so important in powder to maintain speed, especially on flatter sections of the run. Once you slow down or stop in deep powder it is difficult to start up again unless you are on a steep slope – the board sinks with less momentum and floats with more speed.

Remember that even on a sunny day riding in powder you are going to become wet and cold after a couple of tumbles if you aren't wearing the correct gear. The objective here is to keep the snow out of those areas such as your neck.

Powder makes snowboarding seem very easy, but it can be dangerous, with deep snow drifts and hidden hazards. To avoid the board sinking into the soft snow, it is important to maintain speed, especially on the flatter sections of the run. You will also get wet, so wear the correct gear!

Extreme Snowboarding

What is extreme snowboarding? It is the minority of snowboarders that have the chance, capability or the guts to ride in really extreme terrain. Most people will be content to watch these fearless riders on video from the comfort of their living room. Nick Perata has been described as the original extreme rider, having spent many years riding in Alaska and now organizing the World Extreme Championships held in Alaska. Here, Nick gives us an insight into the world of extreme snowboarding.

'Snowboarding is the most fulfilling of all disciplines because all at once you can be free, you can be scared to death and you can go as fast as humanly possible. Extreme snowboarding challenges the rider, not only physically but, maybe even more so, mentally. The outcome of the run and the fate of the rider are based on the individual's decisions regarding his line and speed. Thus, the rider must think a little more when riding extreme terrain, than in other disciplines of snowboarding.

Extreme snowboarding is a lot like golf. The golfer has to take into account everything in his surroundings such as the lie of the ball, the wind, trees, water, sand etc. When riding extreme terrain there are also things to be taken into account such as the steepness of the slope, the snow conditions, rocks, wind, the fall-line, the run out etc.

Since the terrain of extreme snowboarding is more demanding than the groomed ski area, there are certain things to be aware of:

Your own ability. Do not kid yourself. Be honest about your ability. Know your mental and physical limitations in order to stay alive. Do not ride beyond your ability in extreme terrain.

Your surroundings. Know the snow conditions, is it stable? Check for obstacles in your intended line and make sure that the run out of any jump is clean.

Avalanche danger. Avalanches kill, and can occur without warning. Make sure that you are aware of any danger in the area that you are riding. You should be familiar with tests to check the snow's stability and should always ride with an experienced guide. Wear a transceiver (peeps) at all times and be sure that everyone in your party has one.

The pros and cons of extreme riding:

PROS
Incredible Powder
Insane speed
Diversity of challenging terrain
Long exhilarating runs

CONS
Unridable ice
Nasty slams
High risk of injury or death
After a long run, what seems like an even longer hike back up again

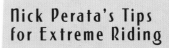

Nick Perata's Tips for Extreme Riding

- Always carefully assess your intended line before committing to the drop.
- Always know what is under the snow ahead.
- Begin with easy terrain or small cliffs and slowly work your way up to bigger things.
- Stick everything!

The best tip that I could give any rider is to ALWAYS REMAIN IN CONTROL. Your life depends on it.'

Extreme snowboarding is one of the most fulfilling, and challenging, of all disciplines. It combines elements of freedom, speed and terror in equal amounts, and should only be attempted once you are a skilled rider and when both physically and mentally prepared.

The Competition Circuit

Competition has always been a part of snowboarding, even if it was just between friends to see who could go the fastest or highest. Nowadays, competitions range from local ski area events to state, national and world championships and are soon to be included in the Olympics. Every discipline is covered – Half pipe, Slopestyle, Boardercross, Slalom, Dual Slalom, Giant Slalom and Extreme Riding. Every country has its own circuit, some amateur, some professional, some on snow, some on artificial slopes of plastic.

HALF PIPE – In a half pipe competition, each rider takes two runs, the scores of which are combined to arrive at a total number of points. Normally there will be a large number of competitors, so the field is reduced by eliminating all but the top 20 or so riders after the first two runs. The qualifying riders fight it out in the final

where a further two runs are judged in order to produce the winner. When scoring, the judges take into account the height of the trick, style, fluidity, difficulty, variety and the number of mistakes or falls.

SLOPESTYLE – This discipline is judged using similar criteria to the half pipe. Instead of using a pipe to perform tricks however, the competitors are provided with a number of hits, jumps and obstacles that would normally be found in a snowboard park. These would include table tops, transfers, quarter pipes, rail slides, drums and cars.

BOARDERCROSS – To make slalom racing more of a fun event and appealing to freestylers as well as racers, boardercross courses were designed. Similar to moto-cross (motorbikes), competitors race together down a course which combines jumps, gaps, banks and turns. The first rider to

the finish line wins. The competition is run in heats of 4 riders, eliminating a number from every heat, until the final 4 remain.

SLALOM – Very similar to the ski racers slalom course, although the gates in a snowboard slalom course are set slightly further apart to account for the snowboards different turning characteristics. The object is to complete the course in a quicker time than all the other riders. Slalom is the most technical of all the competitive disciplines. Racers must be 100% focused on their objective and must know that the slightest mistake will cost them the fastest time. High tech equipment is used and the top few riders are often separated by only a few hundredths of a second – perhaps down to the right choice of wax. Slalom boards are used, around 150 – 160 cm in length, for the fast and tight turns.

DUAL SLALOM – An exciting version of the slalom race, from both the spectators and the racers point of view. Using two identical and parallel slalom courses, riders race against each other and the clock. Each rider races each course and the fastest combined time wins. In the case of a tie, a third run is taken. There will probably be two pro jumps in the course adding further excitement. Again it is ultra important to be focused and small mistakes can lose you the race. However, there are two races and one of the racers can easily give away the second leg after winning the first convincingly. Racing

Left: Boardercross is a fun event that appeals to freestylers as well as racers.

against another rider like this produces a great deal of adrenaline and often pushes individuals further than racing against an invisible clock. The winner does not necessarily have the fastest time of the day but does have the coolest head!

GIANT SLALOM – A longer version of the slalom course where the gates are set much further apart, at least 30 feet. Longer GS boards (160 – 170 cm long) are used as speeds are higher and turns wider than the slalom course. Racers will wear skin suits in order to cut down wind resistance and helmets to guard against injuries resulting from high speed falls. The rider with the fastest time wins. The right line down the course is imperative to success as is being able to carve the board in the prevailing snow conditions. After a number of racers have departed, the course begins to become icy and faster, but more difficult to hold an edge on. Since Super Giant Slalom races are no longer held for snowboarders, the Parallel version of Giant Slalom has been added to many competitions around the world, adding further high speed excitement for both spectators and the riders.

EXTREME – Perhaps the most breathtaking of all the competitive disciplines are the Extreme competitions. The Extreme World Championships are held in Alaska in terrain that can only be reached by helicopters. Judges view the riders runs through binoculars from a position near the base of the allotted competition area. The competition is divided up into 3 days with Ballistic, Extreme and Soul Style making up the judging categories. This is not really a spectator event but the whole contest is filmed and available each year on video for all to see and watch in awe.

Organization

Formed in May 1991, the International Snowboard Federation (ISF) is the governing body for snowboarding worldwide. They are responsible for organizing the ISF World Championships, the ISF World Tour, the Nations Cup, the ISF Junior World Championships and for pushing the International Olympic Committee into accepting snowboarding in the 1998 Olympics in Nagano.

The International Snowboard Association (ISA) represents the European Nations, developing snowboarding on a national level through public relations, media work and organizing competitions.

Every country has its own governing body. Check the back of this book for the main addresses.

Above: A snowboard slalom is the most technical of all the competitive disciplines and the top few riders' times are often separated by fractions of a second.
Below: Dual slalom is an exciting variation of the slalom race, using two parallel courses.

Buying New & Used Equipment

Hopefully by now you have a pretty good idea about the type of snowboard gear that you would like. But how do you go about buying this equipment?

New Gear

Head for your local snowboard store and buy there and then. You can't exactly shop around, can you? There's only one snowboard shop nearby. Maybe they don't have the best selection. Try a ski shop? Some may not really know what they are talking about!

SALES – the cheapest gear will be found at the end of the season. Naturally. If there is any remaining at the beginning of the next season, it will be heavily discounted as it is last year's model. Remember, even though they may never have been used and are as good as new, if gear is a year or so old, it will be outdated and perhaps not such a bargain. The snowboard industry technology is progressing at an alarming rate and you should do your best to keep up.

PACKAGE DEALS – track down stores that put together boards, boots and bindings for lower prices. Generally they are selling gear that they need to move, but it is almost always a good deal.

MAIL ORDER – Sometimes there are some great deals to be found, but obviously you really need to know what you are looking for. Buying boots this way is not a good idea – you need to try them on.

BOOTS – be careful not to buy them too big. Always try to buy boots a size smaller than your street shoes – remember that with use they will stretch. If you buy the boots that feel great walking around the store, more often than not they will be too big and your feet will be swimming after a few weeks of riding, resulting in a lack of board control. Wear thin socks when trying them on in the store. You can always pull out the in-sole at first until they stretch a little.

If you simply cannot afford new boots, then go for the used option. But remember that a boot stretches and moulds to one's foot. So the used boot that you buy will have been shaped to someone else's foot already. It will also have stretched so don't worry about buying a size smaller than normal. Buy a used board, but try to buy new boots if possible. They are the connection between you and the board. If your feet hurt then your riding suffers. Period.

FOOT BEDS – A must for all riders. Foot beds are custom made in-soles that support your foot and increase your level of performance and ride comfort by giving you something to stand on that is the same shape as the sole of your foot, instead of standing on the flat base of the boot interior – more than anything else it's good for your health! Performance wise, they give you a better boot fit, provide added 'feel' for board control and prevent your feet from sliding within the boot. They are available at most ski shops and you just gotta have 'em!

Used Equipment

Ex-demo gear. All manufacturers produce demo equipment for stores and reps. Sometimes the gear is top quality but often it is not. Take your chances if you decide to buy such gear – if you are buying from used sources (ie bulletin boards, newspapers, sponsored riders)

Head for your local snowboard store.

Below: If possible, try to buy new boots . Remember that they will stretch with use, so buy a pair that are a size smaller than your street shoes. (K2 Snowboards)

you will come across ex-demo's. You could be lucky and score a great deal.

Used gear. Whenever and wherever you find used boards, there are some things to look out for.

BOARDS – check the camber, is there any left? Check the side walls and edges – are they intact and not cracked or loose? Remove the bindings. Check the inserts – are they solid? Make sure they have not been pulled out or stripped. Is the top sheet cracked at all? Does the base have bad damage? Is it clean? Are the tip and tail smashed? Does the base look as though it has been regularly serviced?

BINDINGS – Bindings take a lot of punishment, especially on rental boards. Check for any cracks, missing nuts and bolts and straps. Straps also crack and break easily. Make sure the entire set-up is complete. Strap yourself in to check that everything works. Spring loaded catches are likely to be broken.

Buy the best equipment that you can afford, particularly if you anticipate progressing quickly.

Equipment Care & Servicing

There is a huge difference between riding a snowboard that is well serviced and riding a board that has never seen a file or any wax. A board that has sharp edges and is well waxed will perform infinitely better than one that is not. Sharp edges help turning, especially on hard pack snow and in icy conditions. With dull edges, carving will not be easy on hard snow as the board will 'slide out'. A good coat of wax will keep the board sliding in all conditions, even wet snow. No wax on the base results in the board sticking on the snow, making riding more difficult in all but very dry snow. Wax also prolongs the life of the board – the P-Tex base is similar to your skin. It will dry up and crack when dry and needs 'moisturizing'.

If you look after your snowboard by servicing it regularly, it will perform better (so will you!), last longer and have a higher resale value.

TOOLS REQUIRED

- Plastic wax scraper
- Metal P-Tex scraper
- De-burring stone
- De-tuning block
- Surform
- Selection of files
- Edge filing device
- Sharp knife
- Wire brush
- Lighter
- Scrubbing brush
- Iron
- Copper brush
- Nylon brush
- Selection of screw drivers and wrenches
- Duct tape (the solution to every problem in life!)

Look after your snowboard and service it regularly, and it will last longer, perform better and maintain its resale value.

Servicing Your Board

Depending on the particular board in question and its set up, it may be necessary to remove the bindings to achieve a perfect result. Also, some clamps and vices work better if the bindings are removed. Removing the bindings periodically is a good idea anyway so that the inserts can be checked and lubricated.

First, clamp the board face down to a secure workbench.

1. Clean the base and edges with a detergent cleaner. If the base is very dirty with ingrained oil and tar from the lifts, you may need to use a stiff scrubbing brush with the detergent.
2. Check the edges for burs (jagged metal) or any other damage. Burs will ruin a file if they are not removed before the tuning stage. Using an edge grinding stone, remove any burs from the side of the edge only. Be sure to keep the stone flat so as not to alter the angle of the edge. Burs on the base of the edge should be removed with a bastard file. Using a stone on the base edge will damage the P-Tex. Always keep the file flat on the base and always file from the tip of the board towards the tail.
3. Once the edges have been de-burred, they should be sharpened. Tools are available that hold the file at the correct angle for edge sharpening. These are an important part of your tool kit. They are particularly useful for sharpening the side edge. Run the file from tip to tail of the board.

4. The base of the edge should be sharpened using a regular flat file. Keep the file flat on the base at all times and run from tip to tail.

5. Use your nail to check the sharpness of the edge. The most important area of the edge is under the bindings, (ie the centre section of the edge) where most of the turning pressure occurs. This section should always be kept sharp.

6. After sharpening the entire edge, the tip and tail should be de-tuned. If the tip and tail sections of the edges are left sharp, they will catch when riding and impair board control. A de-tuning stone should be used to de-tune the end sections of both edges. The amount of edge that you de-tune depends on the type of board, its use and your personal preference.

7. If there are holes and gouges in the base, they should be filled. Small scratches will not hold any P-Tex, it will simply peel out, so they should be left. They will either disappear when the base is flat filed or will be filled during the hot wax process.

8. Clean away any loose P-Tex with a knife and wire brush. The wire brush also gives the area a key to which the new P-Tex can bond.

9. If you have a specialized P-Tex gun, then applying the P-Tex to the damaged area is easy. Over load the hole so that there is an excess of P-Tex which can be filed down flush with the base. If you do not have the luxury of using a P-Tex gun, you will have to revert to the basic home repair method. You will need a lighter, a metal scraper and a stick of P-Tex (colour dependent on the colour of the base). Place the scraper on the base next to the hole to be repaired – this will catch any unwanted P-Tex drips.

10. Holding the P-Tex stick close to the scraper, light the lower end. Keep the stick as close to the scraper as possible until it is burning well. If you maintain a blue flame, there will be little or no carbon build. When the P-Tex burns with a yellow flame, it is too high above the scraper and burning too much oxygen and will create black carbon, ruining an otherwise perfect repair job.

11. Once the P-Tex begins to drip or run off the stick, move it horizontally until it is over the repair and drip the P-Tex into the hole until it is above the level of the base. You may have to add more at a later stage once the P-Tex has cooled and contracted into the hole.

12. Once all the holes and gouges are filled, the next step is to remove the excess P-Tex. Begin with the metal scraper and/or bastard file, downgrading to the smoothest and the final stage. Use a surform at first then different grades of flat file until you are down to the finest file.

13. By this time the repair should be flush with the base – you should not be able to feel any blemishes.

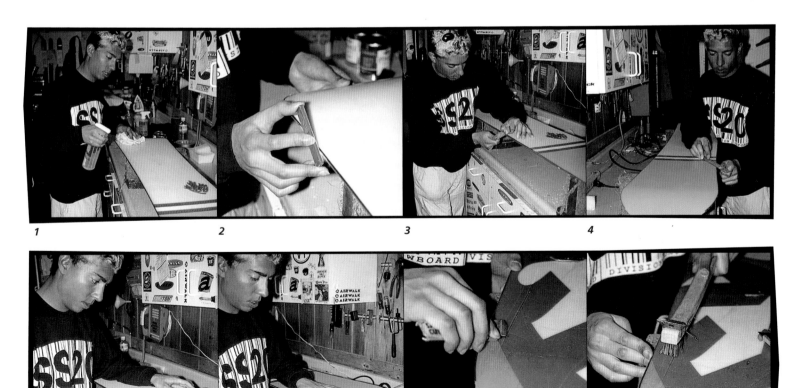

1   2   3   4

5   6   7   8

9   10   11   12

13   14   15   16

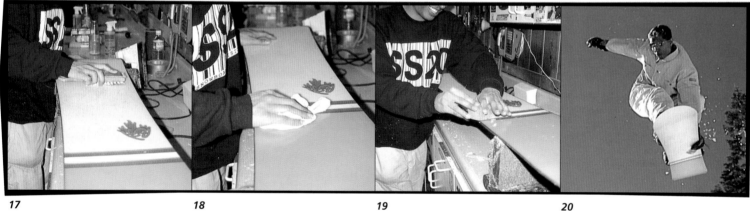

17   18   19   20

Using a flat edge of some kind, check to see if the base is level and flat. Once the base and the edges have been serviced many times, it will be necessary to have the base ground by machine to return it to its original flat state. If you begin servicing your board from new, you can keep the base flat by flat-filing any high spots whenever necessary. Always file from the tip of the board to the tail in order to align the base fibres in one direction, ie the direction that the board is going to slide

on the snow. Now you should have sharp edges and a flat, gouge free base. **14.** The next and final step is to wax the base. First clean the entire base and edges thoroughly to remove any old wax, dirt and metal filings. The type of wax that you use depends on the temperature of the snow. Unless you are preparing the board for a race, regular all-temperature wax will do fine. Wax is available in rub-on or iron-in form. The most effective way to wax your board for performance and

longevity is the iron in method. Ensure that the base is clean, warm and dry. Use a regular clothes iron (don't plan on using it to iron any of your favourite shirts afterwards!), and drip wax from the block onto the board. **15.** Next simply iron the wax into the board until it has covered the entire base. Do not leave the iron in one place on the base – it will burn. Keep the iron moving quickly over the base to prevent overheating your plank. Allow the wax to completely cool off.

16. Using a plastic scraper, scrape the cooled wax off, from the tip towards the tail of the board. You can't remove too much wax – don't worry, it wasn't a waste of time putting the wax on – the wax that is important has been absorbed into the base of the board. You should end up with a shiny, smooth and slick surface.

17. Next you can structure the waxed base. This is not essential but as you made it this far without falling asleep, you may as well finish the job properly! Structuring creates small grooves in the wax allowing water droplets to move along the base, reducing the suction factor between the snow and the board – and, therefore, increasing speed. Using a nylon or copper brush, work from the tip to the tail. Covering the base once is generally satisfactory.

18. Wipe off the loose wax 'dust' with a clean, dry cloth.

19. Lastly, polish the base, again from tip to tail, using a cork block.

20. Now Go Ride!!

GUARANTEE – Your board's performance will now have significantly improved due to these servicing techniques. If it hasn't, quit skimming and read this section again! Properly!!

WARNING – P-Tex burns the skin very easily and does not help to slow the skin's aging process!! Do not drip P-Tex on yourself! How do you know if a snowboarder services his board regularly? Check his hands and arms for P-Tex burn scars!!

If you take good care of your snowboard and service it regularly, it will pay dividends with your performance. Always check your bindings before you ride, and always take a pocket screwdriver set with you, to tighten screws when out on the mountain.

General Equipment Care

As well as servicing the board itself, there are other rituals to be observed.

● Everyday, before you ride, you should check your bindings for loose nuts and bolts. Binding screws are notorious for becoming loose 'on their own'. If you lose a couple of screws on the mountain because you didn't check them that morning, it could be a long hike back to the lodge.

● Carry a pocket screwdriver set at all times to tighten screws on the mountain.

● Close the binding straps when not riding the board. This will help to prevent straps snapping. Fold in the high backs on freestyle bindings and the bails on plate bindings, again to prevent breakage.

● Store your board flat on the floor if possible to maintain its shape. Do not store near a heater – damage can occur.

● Refrain from hanging the board on the ground to remove snow at the end of the day. Use a brush. Snowboards do not take well to repeated impacts with concrete.

● When travelling with your board, especially on airlines, protect your gear thoroughly. Use a padded snowboard bag and wrap your clothes around the board, particularly the edges. Public transportation employees really dislike your new toy and are very jealous of you travelling to the mountains for all that powder. Don't give them the pleasure of wrecking your trip.

● Pull out your boot liners after every use and dry them in a warm place, not on a heater where they will overheat and burn! If your boot outers are leather, treat them with a recommended waterproofing product.

Where to Snowboard

Snowboarders are not confined to the biggest and most well known ski areas that the world has to offer. In fact, anywhere that there is snow and a slope will do, but if you can travel to a ski resort so much the better. remember that there are still one or two areas that do not allow snowboarding, but these are few and far between.

This map shows those areas that are especially recommended for a snowboard vacation as well as the main ski areas of the world. As you can see, there are some great places to plan a trip to, during any of the twelve months – due to our distinct hemispheres, it is possible to ride every day of the year!

Every country has different types of terrain and, in fact, different types of snow. For example, Australia has smaller mountains with beautiful eucalyptus trees adorning the slopes and a great attitude towards snowboarding. The French Alps have impressive mountains with extreme terrain and some of the best powder. California has amazing lake views, a cross section of terrain and a warmer climate – so lots of sun!

For those of you that live miles away from any mountains, don't despair just yet, for there are other options, such as dry ski slopes and indoor snow slopes. In Britain and some other flat areas of Europe, there are several hundred dry ski slopes made of plastic brush. They do not compare to deep powder, but if it's plastic or nothing . . . ! In the summer there is a National Snowboard Competition Tour in the UK, so there is even an opportunity to compete at slalom and freestyle. Strange as it may seem, there are some excellent British riders who have spent little or no time riding on snow!

One of the latest concepts to be introduced into the leisure industry is the indoor ski slope. Basically it is a big fridge with snow making capabilities, built on a gradient. These were first built in Japan and are now popping up in other parts of the world. With quarter pipes and half pipes planned at these facilities, soon we will see indoor World Championship Snowboard events.

Even if it is not winter in your part of the world, some ski areas operate all year round, as they are located on glaciers. In Europe and North America there are a number of great summer snowboarding areas. To satisfy the year round snowboarder, there are many organized snowboard camps available at these glaciers.

Wherever you decide to go for your snowboarding experience, remember that ideal conditions do not always exist. Sometimes you will be lucky and hit a great week for powder, but more often than not conditions may well be less than perfect. But that is part of the sport. To become a good snowboarder you will need to be able to perform in all conditions and then you will be able to enjoy maximum fun wherever you are! Enjoy – and see you there!

Squaw Valley, California – a wonderful part of the United States to go snowboarding.

Recommended Snowboard Destinations

EAST COAST USA
Maine: Sugar Loaf.
Vermont: Okemo, Stowe, Stratton.

WESTERN USA
California: June Mountain, Kirkwood, Mammoth, Homewood, Squaw Valley.
Colorado: Arapahoe Basin, Breckenridge, Crested Butte, Steamboat Springs, Telluride, Vail.
Oregon: Mt. Bachelor. Mount Hood.
Utah: Brighton Ski Resort, Powder Mountain, Solitude Ski Resort.
Wyoming: Jackson Hole.

WESTERN CANADA
Alberta: Banff, Lake Louise.
British Colombia: Blackcomb, Red Mountain, Whistler.

UK
Scotland: Aviemore (Cairngorms), Glencoe, Glenshee (Grampian) The Lecht (East Cairngorms), Nevis Range,

EUROPE
Austria: Axamer-Lizum, Fieberbrunn, Hintertux, Ischgl, Kaprun, Saalbach-Hinterglemm, Solden,
Finland: Levi, Yllas.
France: Avoriaz, Chamonix, Courchevel, Les Arcs, Les Deux Alpes, Méribel, Serre Chevalier, Tignes, Val D'Isere, Val Thorens.
Germany: Garmisch.
Greece: Parnasos.
Iceland: Reykjavik.
Italy: Courmayeur, La Thule.
Norway: Geilo, Hemsedal.
Spain: Sierra Nevada, Formigal.
Sweden: Are, Funasdalen.
Switzerland: Anzere, Davos, Laax, Leysin, Crans Montana, Saas Fee, Verbier, Zermatt.
Turkey: Uludag

REST OF THE WORLD
Argentina: Valle de las Lajas, Bailoche Cran Catedral.
Australia: Falls Creek, Mt Buller, Mt Kosciusko, Tredo.
Chile: Antillanca, La Burbuja, El Colorado, Terma de Chillan, Portillo, Villarrica/Puccon.
India: Solang.
New Zealand: Remarkable, Cardruna, Coronel Peak, Mt Hutt, Ohau, Porter Heights, Treble Cone.

Snowboarding destination details supplied courtesy of Tony Brown, *Universal Snowboard Guide.*

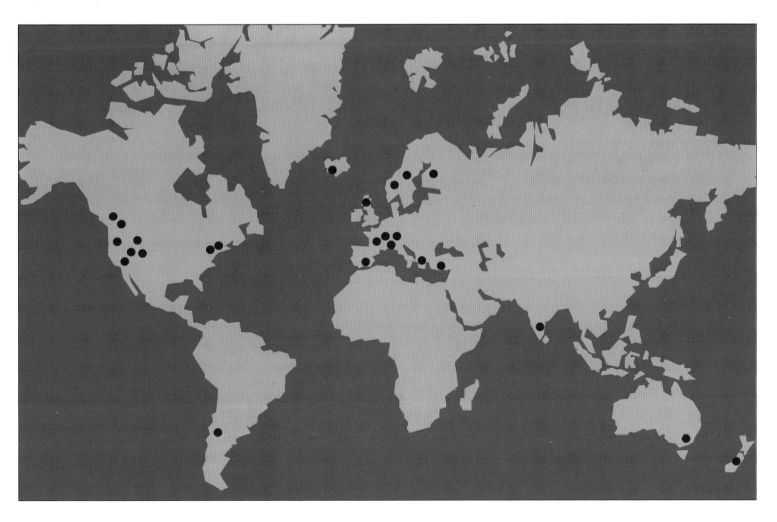

Fitness

Unless you are lucky enough to travel around the world following the winter seasons, you will discover that in the spring time the snow melts to make way for summer. This is great but it means that you have to put your snowboard away for 6 months and do nothing. Or do you?

Pre-season Training

SUMMER TRAINING – In most parts of the world there are glaciers that provide year round snow. On some of the European and North American glaciers, professionally run snowboard camps are organized to provide a summer training venue where riders can learn from the pro's, fine tune their riding and remain in shape for the next winter.

In parts of Europe, particularly Britain, there are hundreds of dry ski slopes that provide another substitute for snow. These slopes are constructed from a plastic bristle and are generally a few hundred feet long with a rope-tow to transport you back to the top. While they may not offer powder conditions, these slopes are a valuable training ground for those riders willing to train over the summer months in preparation for the real thing. Many dry ski slopes have a thriving snowboard club with organized race and freestyle competitions common throughout the summer.

What if you are not able to ride at all? There are many ways to stay fit and to retain the strength and endurance that you gained while snowboarding. Cross-training means that you use a number of different sports to keep fit

and to increase your overall physical strength, balance, endurance and skill. You will become a better snowboarder by practicing other sports that can teach you new skills and by taking part in several activities, rather than just snowboarding, you are less likely to become burnt out or bored. Here are some suggestions for off-snow cross-training sports and the benefits of each:

Mountain Biking – balance, leg strength, endurance, speed control and increased pain threshold!!

Surfing – balance, upper body strength, endurance and a sun tan.

Roller blading – leg strength, speed control, endurance, road rash.

Trampolining – balance, ankle strength – tape up the edges of your board and strap in. Practice those airs!

Weight training – train every muscle group for strength.

Soccer – strength, endurance.

Stretching – very important at all times of the year. For flexibility, strength and to reduce injury.

There are many sports that will help you to keep fit during the summer months when you are not able to ride your snowboard. Surfing (right) and water skiing (below left) will maintain your balance and upper body strength. Weight training or general fitness training at your local gym (below) will help to keep all of your muscles toned up and prepare you for the new season.

Stretching

For some reason stretching is overlooked as an important part of everyday life. For an athlete it is crucial that stretching becomes a daily activity in order to reduce the chances of injury during any of the above sports. For the snowboarder, being flexible is important in order that the body can move freely into all the contorted positions that are snowboarding. Try to set up a daily routine of simple stretches and definitely stretch before riding each day. As well as improving your flexibility, stretching will help to warm up the muscles before you ride – after all, you are about to spend the day in freezing weather exerting more force and tension on your body than at most other times of your life. You need to be fit. The following is a selection of basic stretches designed to increase your performance. There are many more advanced stretching exercises that you should learn as you gain experience.

Neck.

Hamstrings.

Hamstrings.

Hamstrings and groin.

Seated groin.

Wrists.

Calves.

Quadriceps.

Lower back and trunk.

Shoulders.

Safety & Rules of the Slopes

Beginner skiers are taught, as part of their ski lessons, safety and etiquette while on the ski slopes. As just about every learner skier takes lessons due to its difficulty, so every skier becomes aware of the need for 'road rules' on the snow.

Many snowboarders, however, take up the sport without organized lessons as it is relatively simple to learn alone, although this is not advisable. Many of these snowboarders have never skied before and therefore are not conscious of the rules that are made to promote safety on the ski slopes. This is part of the reason that snowboarding received such bad publicity in the early days when many accidents occurred between snowboarders and skiers. No one party was at fault as skiing and snowboarding are such different sports and both use the ski slopes in entirely different fashions. So, until both skiers and snowboarders learn the characteristics of each others sport, there is bound to be a conflict and unnecessary accidents.

Education is the key factor. Skiers need to be educated that snowboarding is not an uncontrollably dangerous sport but that it is as safe as skiing, provided that proper lessons are taken. Snowboards are not toys, they are highly technical winter sports equipment and should be treated accordingly. Snowboarders need to be educated on the rules of the slopes and the correct etiquette and should understand the way in which a skier moves. Skiers also need to learn that snowboards perform differently to skis

and need to be able to anticipate a snowboarders next move.

The following rules provide a guideline to all snowboarders on how to behave on the ski slopes. Remember, skiers were here first and the more we learn to ride by their slope rules, the better life will be for all of us!

Responsibility

Every snowboarder must be responsible for their actions and their safety on the slopes. All snowboarders must be in control of their board at all times and must learn to expect the unexpected, for example, be prepared to take evasive action in order to avoid obstacles or other skiers and snowboarders. Do not snowboard on slopes beyond your capability. Always ride at a speed that corresponds to your level of competence.

Overtaking

When approaching another skier or snowboarder from behind, ie from an up-hill position, responsibility for both groups falls on your shoulders. If you are the up-hill snowboarder and overtaking other people, you have the best view of the situation and are best able to change direction, etc, if need be.

Awareness

The up-hill rider should be aware that everybody snowboards and skis in a

different fashion and therefore may make any number of unexpected moves. There are several different types of people on the mountain – beginner snowboarders, freestyle snowboarders, alpine snowboarders, beginner skiers, alpine skiers, telemark skiers and mono-skiers, to name but a few, and they all use totally different equipment that has different performance characteristics and thus different forms of motion are created. Therefore every snowboarder must learn to recognise the different types of equipment and be able to anticipate the type of movement that could be expected from the operator.

Stopping on the Slope

When stopping on a slope, a snowboarder should always do so as far to the side of the run as possible, staying out of danger. Always stop in a place where you can be seen from further up the slope. Never stop below a jump, below a rise or around a turn in the ski run. When returning back onto the slope, be sure to look up the hill for oncoming snowboarders or skiers. In this instance, the uphill skier/snowboarder has the right of way. If you fall, be sure to get to your feet as soon as possible and move out of the way of oncoming skiers and snowboarders. Refrain from stopping at narrow points on the slope, at junctions of two or more runs or in any place where skiers and snowboarders are moving rapidly. In snowboard parks or around jumps, never stop near or on the take off to a jump. After using a hit or jump, move clear of the landing area as soon as possible to a place that you are visible to the next snowboarder in line.

Hiking

This is especially relevant to snowboarders due to the nature of the sport, particularly freestyle. There are many hits on the ski slopes and on occasion, snowboarders choose to take several runs on the same hit/jump. In this instance it is very important that the snowboarder stays to the side of the ski run when hiking back to the hit, in order that no danger is caused to the skiers and snowboarders on the main slope. The same rule applies, should it be necessary to hike down the slope.

Safety Leashes

If you have ever seen a runaway snowboard on a ski slope, you will be aware that once they have reached cruising speed, they can be classed as a dangerous weapon, capable of causing major damage and injuries. To ensure that your snowboard is never transformed into a skier seeking missile, always wear a leash on your front leg and attach it securely to the front binding. In some ski resorts, particularly in the USA, you will not be allowed on the lifts without a leash. Practice safe snowboarding – always wear a leash!

Respect Slope Signs

When driving a car on the road, there are warning and information signs to be observed. The same applies to the ski slopes which can become congested and sometimes as dangerous as our roads – snowboarders must take note of ALL slope signs. Here are some examples; 'Slow, Trails Merging', 'Experts Only – Double Black Diamond Run', 'Danger, Cliff Area', 'Closed'.

Accidents

If you are present when an accident occurs, it is your duty as a responsible snowboarder to stop and assist in any way possible. If you are involved in an accident or simply witness to one, you are also obliged to leave your name and address with the group at the scene so that you can be contacted regarding the incident.

Enjoy your snowboarding, but learn the rules to ensure that you are safe and courteous.

Skier Courtesy

It is well known that there are still a number of skiers that are anti-snowboarding either due to a certain ignorance of our sport or simply due to stubbornness. Some skiers are also frightened when approached by snowboarders as they are not familiar as to how they perform on the slopes. It can be worrying to skiers, especially beginners, to hear the sound of a snowboarder gaining on them from behind. So, in order to win over the remaining group of people that do not appreciate the presence of snowboarders on the ski slopes, it is imperative that all snowboarders stay courteous to all skiers at all times, whatever the situation. This is essential to the continued rapid growth of snowboarding.

The Future of Snowboarding

Snowboarding continues to produce the freshest and most enterprising product innovations and the riders themselves are pushing forward the level of the sport on a daily basis.

Finally, it seems that snowboarding will be represented in the Olympics. Perhaps all the ski resorts will take note and allow the sport at the remaining few anti-snowboarding establishments. Perhaps even Park City, Utah, who host the Olympics in 2002 will allow snowboarding! As yet, they do not and have no intention of relenting apart from the duration of the competition itself.

Snowboarding is now a major business, forming the mainstay of the winter sports industry. So what about the future? All the projected figures tell us that snowboarding will continue to grow, but what does the industry think? Martin Robinson is the UK distributor of several leading US snowboard products and gives his view of what is in store for all involved with the sport.

'Hardly a day goes by without reference to the ever changing and rapidly evolving world we live in and our leisure activities are no exception. The late '80s and early '90s have seen the emergence of many new, challenging and exciting outdoor action sports. Snowboarding is one of the sports at the forefront of this revolution and is, without doubt, the world's fastest growing winter sport.

The passing of recent years has seen huge advances in equipment technology and performance, clothing design and the evolution of progressive and smooth, fluid riding styles. This has provided the images necessary to make snowboarding appealing to all kinds of people and to assure its growth well into the next millennium. As more and more young people take up snowboarding, together with the increasing adult cross-over from other sporting areas and developing ties within the music and fashion arenas, we can be sure that this is no fad or craze.

Anyone new to the sport will be well aware of the extensive range of hardware and software available, as the industry establishes its manufacturing, distribution and retail structures. Without doubt, the next few years will see a reduction in the number of companies offering products, but this is not peculiar to snowboarding. It will allow a less confusing choice for the consumer, higher quality, better service and lower prices, which is in the best long term interests of this great new winter activity.

With snowboarding now an Olympic sport, it is sure to reach a truly worldwide audience, a sport for all. Many true enthusiasts do not level with the Olympic ideal and the increasing commercialization surrounding it, but snowboarding is an individual, creative, healthy pastime exercised in the natural environment, and is different things to different people.

Ride and enjoy – and who knows, it might just change your life.'

Glossary

Adrenaline: A hormone secreted by the medulla of the adrenal gland giving you a natural high feeling.

Air, getting: The act of becoming airborne.

Alpine: Style of snowboarding using hard boots, bindings and race type snowboard.

All terrain: Snowboard designed for riding all that a mountain can offer.

Angulation: The angle of the board's edge in relation to the snow.

Baggy pants: Snowboarding pants cut large for extra movement.

Base: The underside of the snowboard, generally made of P-Tex.

Beanie: Woollen or fleece hat.

Binding: Device that secures the rider's feet to the snowboard.

Boardercross: Race involving gates, jumps and banks, run with four riders per heat.

Bone: To straighten one leg while performing a trick in the air.

Bonk: To purposely hit an obstacle with the board while airborne.

Breathable: Clothing material that allows excess body heat to escape, preventing sweating.

Burr: Rough section of the edge of a snowboard, caused by contact with rocks, for example.

Button: Type of surface lift that transports one person up the slope.

Camber: The amount of bend measured at the snowboard's waist.

Cap: Type of board construction using a one-piece top and side wall section.

Carbon: Fibre used in some boards as reinforcement.

Carving: Turning the board on edge without sliding, leaving a razor-sharp track in the snow.

Centred: Stance where the distance from the nose to the front binding is the same as the distance from the tail to the rear binding.

Chair lift: Your opportunity to rest while being transported back to the top of the mountain.

Counter rotation: Turning the upper body in the opposite and wrong direction while turning.

Crud: Lumpy, old, unenjoyable snow.

De-burring stone: Product for removing edge roughness.

De-tune: Reduce sharpness of edges at the tip and tail of the board.

Down-weight: Lowering your centre of gravity by bending at the knees, thus applying greater pressure directly to the board's edge.

Duct tape: strong adhesive tape that is a snowboarder's best friend. can be used to fix anything!

Effective edge: The section of the edge that is in contact with the snow, thus affecting the board's performance.

Euro-carvers: Old school European riders that insisted on laying out horizontally on the snow at every turn.

Extreme: Style of riding including cliff-jumps and steep chutes, Big boards and a lot of guts are needed.

Fad: A passing fashion. not snowboarding!

Fakie: Riding backwards.

Fall-line: The path a snowball would take if it rolled down the slope from your position.

Fat: Something that is bigger and better.

Although not as extreme as some cliff-jumps, plunging off any high ridge takes a lot of guts, and is not for the inexperienced rider.

Flat ground: Freestyle tricks performed without the aid of hits on terrain with little slope angle.

Flex pattern: Specific bending characteristics of the snowboard.

Fluorescent: Very bright colours popular in the late '80s, especially with one piece suits.

Foam core: The centre material of the board.

Forward flex: One of the bending characteristics of a hard snowboard boot.

Free-riding: Style of riding where the snowboarder rides the whole mountain incorporating freestyle, carving and powder into everyday cruising.

Freestyle: Style of riding specific to the half pipe, flat ground and airs.

Freestyle refers to the style of riding that includes air tricks such as this tail grab.

Garb: Particularly distinctive fashion or mode of dress.

Gate: Two sets of poles used to mark the turns in slalom and giant slalom.

Giant slalom: Timed race through gates. Longer and faster version of the slalom

Goofy: Riding with the right foot forward.

Half pipe: Tube shaped construction made in the snow for freestyle snowboarding.

Hard binding: Device used to secure hard boots to the snowboard.

Hard pack: Snow that has been compressed to form a solid riding surface. Perfect for carving.

Hard shell boots: Ski type boots used with alpine/race boards for extra precision and control.

Heel edge: The edge of the board closest to the heel of the rider's boots.

Hit: A jump or bank of snow which snowboarders continually launch from.

Horizontal lamination: Method of constructing the core of a snowboard.

Ice: A snowboarder's enemy, unless found in a drink.

Inserts: Steel nuts fixed in the board to which the bindings are screwed.

Invert: A freestyle manoeuvre where the snowboarder turns upside down in the air.

Jib: To purposely hit an obstacle with the snowboard while airborne.

Kevlar: Material used as reinforcement in the construction of some snowboards.

Kicker: Steep jump that helps to propel the rider skyward.

Lateral flex: one of the bending characteristics of a hard snowboard boot.

Layering: Wearing several thin layers of clothing rather than one thick layer.

Learning curve: Graph depicting the progression of a beginner snowboarder.

Leash: Safety strap linking the rider to the board, designed to prevent runaway snowboards.

Lifts: Mechanical device which transports snowboarders back to the top of the mountain.

Lip: Upper edge of a half pipe, bank or wind-blown snow wave.

Medial flex: One of the bending characteristics of a hard snowboard boot.

Mitts: Fingerless gloves.

Moguls: Bumps formed on steeper slopes by continually skiing or snowboarding the same line.

Mono block: Type of board construction using a one piece top sheet and side wall section.

New school: The latest styles and tricks in snowboarding.

Nose: Front end of the snowboard.

Off piste: Anywhere off the groomed slope.

Off ramp: Exit point at the top of a lift.

Ollie: A technique designed to propel both board and rider into the air with or without the use of a hit.

Park: A designated area for snowboarders with quarter pipes, kickers, rail slides etc.

Plate binding: Device to secure hard boots to a snowboard.

Powder: Fresh, deep, light snow with low moisture content that provides the ultimate riding experience.

P-Tex: Type of plastic used as base material on most snowboards.

Quarter pipe: Literally one half of a half pipe, natural or man-made for freestyle tricks.

Quips: A smart, sarcastic comment or observation.

Rail slide: A wooden or metal bar or a fallen tree that can be ridden on a snowboard.

Regular: Riding with the left foot forwards.

Rip: To ride aggressively or in an impressive manner.

Shovel: The scoop of the snowboard's nose.

Side cut: The curve of the snowboard's edge.

Side slip: Travelling down the slope's fall-line by sliding on one edge only, board pointing across the fall-line.

Skate: Using your rear foot to push yourself around on flat terrain, front foot in the binding.

Slalom: Timed race through close spaced sets of poles.

Slam: To fall hard while riding.

Slope style: Judged competition involving jumps, quarter pipes and rail slides.

Soft binding: Device used to secure soft boots to the board.

Soft boots: Flexible boots mainly used for freestyle/freeriding providing essential freedom and movement.

Speed: One of your best friends.

SPF: Skin Protection Factor of sunscreen.

Stance: The riding position.

Steel edges: Sharp metal component of the snowboard, enabling turns to be made on hard pack or ice.

Step in: Type of binding that the boot simply clips into, without straps and buckles.

Stiffy: Straightening both legs while performing a trick in the air.

Stomp pad: Non-slip rubber glued on board between the bindings to give traction to rear foot.

Switch stance: Riding the board and performing tricks backwards.

Tail: Back end of the snowboard.

Tail kick: Up-turned section at the rear of the board.

T-bar: Type of surface lift that will drag two people at once up the slope.

Tip: Front end of the snowboard.

Toe edge: The edge of the board closest to the toe of the rider's boots.

Transition: Curve of a hit or half pipe connecting the horizontal section to the vert.

Traverse: To ride across the slope's fall-line on one edge.

Twin tip: Type of snowboard which has an identical nose and tail design. For freestyle.

Un-weight: Releasing the pressure on the board's edge by flexing the body upwards from the knees.

Upper body: Head, shoulders, arms and hips.

UV: (Ultra Violet) Rays of light that can damage your skin and eyes and should be protected against.

Vert: Steepest section of a hit or half pipe, above the transition.

Vertical lamination: Method of constructing the core of a snowboard.

Waist: Narrowest part of the snowboard.

Wax: Product applied to the base of the board to increase its sliding properties and its life.

Wood core: Centre construction of a snow board.

Wrap around edges: Steel edges continuing around the board's tip and tail for added durability.

Slalom is a timed race, through sets of poles.

Useful Addresses

Organizing Bodies

INTERNATIONAL
ISF Europe – Burgerstrasse 17/11,
A-6020 Innsbruck, Austria.
Tel: 43.512.563890
Fax: 43.512.563890.9
ISF N.America – P.O Box 477, Vail,
CO 81658
Tel: 303.949.5673
Fax: 303.949.4949

NATIONAL
USA – USASA, Box4400, Frisco, CO
80443
Tel: 303.6683350
CANADA – CFS, Sainte-Foy PQ G1V
2x3, 2440 de Prevel 4
Tel: 418 6889781
UK – BSA, 5 Cressex Rd, High
Wycombe, Bucks HP12 5PG
Tel: 01494 462225
FRANCE – AFS, 19 Rue de Dijon, Nice
06000
Tel: 93880880
AUSTRIA – ASA, Brauhausgasse 7,
Himbergl, 2325
Tel: 02235 87494
GERMANY – DSDV, Postfach 120327,
Munchen, 80031
Tel: 089 8958081
AUSTRALIA – NSW-SA, 22 Battle St,
Balmain 2042, NSW
Tel: 02 8185047

OTHERS
ALASKA FREERIDING FEDERATION –
AFFI, 8320 Resurrection Drive,
Anchorage, Alaska 99504
Tel: 907 333 4998

General Addresses

BURTON SNOWBOARDS
80 Industrial Parkway
Burlington, VT, 05401 USA
Tel: (802) 862 4500

SECOND LEVEL SPORT LTD
Clockhouse Lane, Bedfont, Feltham
Middx TW14 8QA, UK
Tel: 01784 251000
Fax: 01784 247169

K2 SNOWBOARDS
19215 Vashon Highway S.W. Vashon Is
WA 98070 USA
Tel: (800) 972 4038
Fax: (206) 463 8254

SURF MOUNTAIN
146 Chiswick High Road
London W4 1PU, UK
Tel: 0181 994 6769

CHALET SNOWBOARD LTD
(Specialist Snowboarding Holidays)
31 Aldworth Avenue, Wantage, Oxon
OX12 7EJ, UK
Tel/fax: 01235 767182

THE SNOWDOME
Leisure Island, River Drive, Tamworth,
Staffs B79 7ND, UK
Tel: 01827 67905

Further Reading

SNOWBOARDER MAGAZINE
Box 1028, Dana Point, CA 92629 USA
Tel: (717) 496 5922
Fax: (714) 496 7849

TRANSWORLD SNOWBOARDING
PO Box 469019, Escondido CA 92046-
9019 USA
Tel: (619) 745 2809

WHITELINES MAGAZINE
Permanent Publishing, 2-2A The Bridge
Centre, Bridge St, Abingdon Oxon
OX14 3HN, UK
Tel: 01235 536 229

SNOWBOARD UK
Air Publications, Unit 1A, Franchise St,
Kidderminster, Worcs DY11 6RE, UK
Tel: 01562 827744

ONBOARD EUROPEAN
SNOWBOARDING MAGAZINE
Spielbergstrasse 1, Fieberbrunn in Tirol,
A-6391, Austria
Tel: 43 (0) 5354 6303

UNIVERSAL SNOWBOARDING GUIDE
Ice Publishing, 45 Corrour Rd,
Dalfaber, Aviemore, Inverness-shire
PH22 1SS, UK
Tel/fax: 01479 810 362

The Internet

MOUNTAINZONE E-ZINE
live reports on snowboarding events
and contests can be found at
www.mountainzone.com

Index

Accessories 28
Accidents 88, 89
Alpine 35, 36
American Sports Data Demographics (ASDD) 14
Avalanche 72

Back pack 29
Balance exercises 39-43
Base 20
Beanie 24, 27
Bindings 22, 36, 77, 81
   alpine 23
   freestyle 23
   step-in 23
Board bag 29, 81
Board design 18
Boardercross 74
Board lock 29
Boards 16, 76, 77
   alpine 19
   freestyle 19, 34, 35
   half pipe 19
   powder 20
   race 19, 35
   servicing 78-81
Board-skiing 12
Bonking 32
Boots 22, 76

Camber 18, 58
Carpenter, Jake Burton 8
Carving 58
Clothing 24
Competition 74, 75, 82
Computer Aided Design (CAD) 16
Conflict, with skiing 12
Courtesy 89

Dry ski slope 82, 84

Edge 20
Effective edge 20
Etiquette 13, 88
Eurocarve 60
Extreme 72, 74, 75

Fakie 32, 36, 46, 60
Fall, how to 38
Falling leaf 44, 47
Fitness 84
Fleece 26
Flex 18, 58
Foot centring 37
Freeriding 34
Freestyle 32, 36, 60

Garlands 44, 48, 52
Gelfand, Alan 62
Glacier 82
Gloves 27
Goggles 28
Goofy 36

Half pipe 30, 31, 35, 74, 82
Hats 27
Heel anchors 29
Heel edge 39
Heelside turn 40, 41, 53, 54, 55, 58
Hiking 89
Hip pack 29

Intermediate turn 55, 58
   linked 55

Jackets 26
Jibbing 32
Jumps 64

Leash 38, 89
Lens cloth 28
Lift 50
   chair 51
   drag 50
   unloading 50, 51
Lip balm 29

Milovich, Dimitrije 10
Mini tool 29
Mono-block 16
Mono-boarding 12
Mountain biking 84

Neck warmer 24, 27
'New school' 32
Nollie 32, 62
Nose shovel 19, 34

Ollie 18, 32, 62, 64

Olympics 7, 74, 75, 90
Overtaking 88

Pants 27, 38
Perata, Nick 7, 72
'Pipe dragon' 31
Poppen, Sherman 8
Powder 34, 36, 64, 70-71, 82
Power straps 29
P-Tex 16, 78, 79, 81

Quarter pipe 31, 82

Racing 35
Regular 36
Roller blading 84

Safety 88
Side cut 18, 34, 35, 58
Side slipping 44, 45, 46, 48, 52, 53, 54, 55
Signs 89
Sims, Tom 8
Skiboard 10, 12
Slalom 35, 74
   dual 74
   giant 35, 74, 75
Slide turn 52
Slopestyle 74
Snowskis 10
Snow-surfing 12
Snurfer 8, 12
'Spec Savers' 28
Stance, riding 36, 37, 42, 51, 52
Stomp pads 29

Stopping 44, 88
Strapping in 38
Stretching 37, 84, 86-87
Surfing 84
Sunglasses 28
Sun screen 28
Sweater 26

Tail 20
Tail kick 19
T-bar 50
Techniques 36-73
Thermals 26
Tobogganing 12
Toe blocks 29
Toe edge 39
Toeside turn 40, 41, 52, 53, 54, 55
Training 84
Trampolining 84
Traverses 44
   linked 52
   skidded 46, 47
Tricks 66
   freestyle 66-69
   flat ground 66

Ultra Violet (UV) 28

Vitelli, Serge 60

Waist 20
Wax 80
Weber, Bob 10
Weight training 84
'Winterstick' 10

Inspired by Jonno's expert advice, the Parragon team take to their snowboards. Thanks to the invaluable text and step-by-step pictures, they all became experts, despite Richie Keary's appalling instructional techniques and having to listen to Kahuna – the world's worst bar-room singer.